DOS 6.2

SIMPLIFIED

Rod B. Southworth

Laramie County Community College

COURSE
TECHNOLOGY

ONE MAIN STREET, CAMBRIDGE, MA 02142

an International Thomson Publishing company I(T)P®

Cambridge • Albany • Bonn • Boston • Cincinnati • London • Madrid • Melbourne • Mexico City
New York • Paris • San Francisco • Singapore • Tokyo • Toronto • Washington

Credits:

Acquisitions Editor: Anne Hamilton
Production Editor: Jean Bermingham
Production Services: GEX, Inc.
Interior Design: Jean Hammond
Cover Art: Diana Coe
Manufacturing Coordinator: Tracy Megison

© 1995 by Course Technology.
A Division of International Thomson Publishing – I(T)P®

For more information contact:

Course Technology
One Main Street
Cambridge, MA 02142

International Thomson Publishing Europe
Berkshire House 168-173
High Holborn
London WCIV 7AA
England

Thomas Nelson Australia
102 Dodds Street
South Melbourne, 3205
Victoria, Australia

Nelson Canada
1120 Birchmount Road
Scarborough, Ontario
Canada M1K 5G4

International Thomson Editores
Campos Eliseos 385, Piso 7
Col. Polanco
11560 Mexico D.F. Mexico

International Thomson Publishing GmbH
Königswinterer Strasse 418
53227 Bonn
Germany

International Thomson Publishing Asia
211 Henderson Road
#05-10 Henderson Building
Singapore 0315

International Thomson Publishing Japan
Hirakawacho Kyowa Building, 3F
2-2-1 Hirakawacho
Chiyoda-ku, Tokyo 102
Japan

Trademarks
Course Technology and the open book logo are registered trademarks and CourseKits is a trademark of Course Technology. Custom Editions is a registered trademark of International Thomson Publishing.

I(T)P® The ITP logo is a registered trademark of International Thomson Publishing.

Some of the product names and company names used in this book have been used for identification purposes only and may be trademarks or registered trademarks of their respective manufacturers and sellers.

Disclaimer
Course Technology reserves the right to revise this publication and make changes from time to time in its content without notice.

ISBN 0-87709-628-7

Printed in the United States of America

10 9 8 7 6 5 4 3

CONTENTS

DOS 6.2 Simplified is ideally suited for use in any formal educational or training environment, or for self-study. The book was written with a one- or two-credit DOS 6 course in mind, but it is equally appropriate as a supplementary book in any course that introduces DOS commands.

No previous experience with DOS is required to use this book. However, students who gain the most from it are those who have already experienced frustration when trying to use DOS effectively.

OBJECTIVES OF THIS BOOK

The objectives of this book are:

- To provide readers with a fundamental overview of the components of personal computer systems.

- To introduce readers to the concepts of using an operating system.

- To simplify the understanding of those commands most frequently used and their associated options.

- To show how to use both the command line and the DOS shell to execute DOS commands, including commands in Version 6.2.

- To improve readers' ability to use personal computers effectively through minimized keystrokes, improved disk and memory management, and customized execution of computer processes.

- To give users the necessary foundation of knowledge to continue learning DOS on their own.

DISTINGUISHING FEATURES

Simplifies Using DOS

To accommodate the different backgrounds and expertise of students using this book, topics in this text are presented logically, one step at a time. A summary of objectives begins each chapter; information is then built upon as the chapter develops. The carefully constructed examples of DOS in action help readers become more self-sufficient personal computer users.

Focuses on Frequently Used DOS Commands

This textbook features step-by-step instruction on the most frequently used DOS commands and their associated options. It is designed to help readers gain better understanding and control of personal computers through the efficient use of DOS.

Distinguishes Between Internal and External DOS Commands

In the early chapters internal and external DOS commands are presented separately to help readers understand the differences between these types of commands. Later in the text, DOS commands are presented by functional use.

Covers Hard Disk versus Floppy Disk Environments

In keeping with the current trend in personal computer instruction, this book emphasizes the hard disk environment, but also addresses the floppy disk environment. Examples of DOS commands and lab exercises are given for both environments. For labs using only floppy disks, the Instructor's Manual provides instructions for configuring a floppy disk to imitate a hard disk environment.

Uses the Command Line and the DOS Shell

Knowing how to enter DOS commands at the system prompt is very helpful. Sometimes it is a necessity for using the DOS shell. Thus, primary emphasis is placed on entering commands from the command line. Where applicable, command line examples are followed by examples using the DOS shell for comparison. The shell is introduced early in this text (Chapter 4). It is covered in specific sections that can be bypassed, if desired. The reader (or the instructor) may decide which approach is preferred.

Emphasizes DOS Structure

An overall understanding of the structure of DOS is essential in effective computer use. This text's thorough coverage of disk organization and management teaches readers to effectively use the computer system with increased efficiency.

Covers Advanced DOS Usage

The advanced topics in this text include customizing DOS, memory management, and advanced batch files. The advanced DOS commands covered include DEFRAG, DBLSPACE, DELTREE, FDISK, MODE, MEM, MEMMAKER, MSBACKUP, MSD, MSAV, PRINT, SCANDISK, SET, SETVER, SMARTDRV, and SYS.

Features Class-tested Exercises for Floppy and Hard Disks

Each chapter includes a substantial set of student-tested exercises. These exercises build on material learned from previous chapters, and also include new material contained in each chapter. Some exercises are included in the body of the text for immediate reinforcement, and others are at the end of each chapter. Most chapters contain separate exercises for floppy disk and hard disk systems.

Uses Actual Screen Illustrations

DOS commands are illustrated with screen "dumps" that accurately reflect what users' screens will look like as they execute target commands. The screen illustrations provide users with visual verification, which highlights the impact of each operation performed.

Proven Material

This text has evolved from the collective experience of the instructors and students who have shared their comments and suggestions. Every attempt was made to preserve the integrity of those elements that proved effective and to improve those that did not.

Instructor's Support Material

An Instructor's Manual featuring additional student exercises, helpful teaching suggestions, answers to chapter review questions, and a large set of class-tested, multiple-choice test questions is available for use by adopters of this text. Instructors should contact South-Western Publishing Company or their local boyd & fraser representative to request this supplementary material.

ACKNOWLEDGMENTS

This book would not have been possible without the guidance, help, and advice of many supportive individuals. To the many reviewers I offer my thanks for providing valuable contributions during the book's development:

Susan Beal
Louisiana State University

Floyd Leach
University of California at Riverside

Peter Chase
Sul Ross State University

Geetha Murthy
Harper College

Roy W. Hedrick
University of South Carolina

Roger Stone
Northern Montana College

Ronald E. Johnson
Vatterott College

I especially thank Patrice Gapen for her encouragement and support. I also thank the students and faculty at Laramie County Community College, who had faith in my material and never failed to make valuable comments about whatever they did and did not like. The entire staff at boyd & fraser, especially Anne Hamilton and Jean Bermingham, did a remarkable job of editing and producing this book. To all these people, I remain indebted for their efforts.

Rod B. Southworth
Cheyenne, Wyoming
February 1994
Prodigy ID: SPGJ85A
Internet: lcrsouth@antelope.wcc.edu

INTRODUCTION TO PERSONAL COMPUTERS

HARDWARE

The Central Processing Unit (CPU)

Primary Storage (RAM)

Input/Output Devices

Secondary Storage

SOFTWARE

Application Software

System Software

INTRODUCTION TO PERSONAL COMPUTERS

Chapter 1 gives an overview of the basic components of personal computers, or PCs. Students using this text undoubtedly have varying degrees of PC experience and knowledge; this chapter provides a common framework of concepts and terminology related to IBM and IBM-compatible PCs.

This chapter covers the two major parts of all PC systems: hardware and software. Having a good understanding of these basics will simplify the learning of DOS, the Disk Operating System for IBM and IBM-compatible PCs.

When you purchase a PC, you may have to make choices about the power of the CPU (central processing unit) and the types of input, output, and storage devices needed. The information presented in this chapter will aid you in making these choices.

HARDWARE

Hardware refers to the physical components of a computer system. Typically, hardware includes four categories: the central processing unit (CPU), primary storage (RAM), input/output devices, and secondary storage devices. Figure 1.1 summarizes the various PC hardware parts discussed in this chapter.

Figure 1.1
PC Hardware

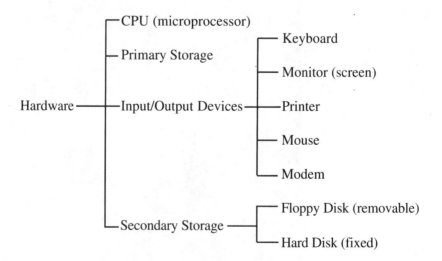

The Central Processing Unit (CPU)

The **central processing unit**, or **CPU**, is described as the "heart" of a computer system because it controls all activities within the system. The CPU is usually one of the five **microprocessor** chips designed by Intel Corporation: the 8088, 80286,

80386, 80486, or Pentium (586). Each of these microprocessor chips has different capabilities related primarily to speed and processing power. Generally, the higher the chip's number, the faster and more powerful its capabilities.

All computer circuits, including microprocessors, function in one of two states: on or off. Symbolically, the on condition is represented with the value 1 and the off condition with the value 0. These two values are **binary digits**, or **bits**. Groups of bits combine to represent characters that store data on a computer. A character is a number (0–9), an alphabetic letter (A–Z), or a special symbol such as an asterisk, dollar sign, or decimal point. For example, the bit pattern 01000001 represents the uppercase letter A.

A **binary item** or **byte** is a group of 8 bits, representing a single character. Many earlier computers were "byte machines." However, it is more efficient to work with more than one character at a time. When bytes are grouped (always in multiples of two), the addressable groups are called **words**. A 16-bit word represents two characters, a 32-bit word represents four characters, and so on. Word machines access and transfer characters faster than do byte machines. The original IBM PC, which used the 8088 microprocessor chip, had a 16-bit internal word structure with an 8-bit path for transfer of input and output data. The newer microprocessor chips process many more bits at a time (Figure 1.2).

All microprocessor chips use a **clock rate** that determines the frequency of the internal operations and keeps everything in proper synchronization. The need for an internal clock is analogous to the need for a conductor at a symphony to control the beat. The faster the clock runs, the faster the computer can process data and instructions. Clock rates are measured in units called **megahertz (MHz)**, a term for one million cycles per second. The internal clock speed of the 8088 chip is a relatively slow 4.77 MHz. Figure 1.2 identifies the major differences in commonly used microprocessor chips.

Figure 1.2
Microprocessor Chips in PCs

CHIP TYPE	CLOCK SPEED (MHz)	INTERNAL DATA PATH (bits)	EXTERNAL DATA PATH (bits)
8088	4.77	16	8
80286	8-16	16	16
80386SX	16-25	32	16
80386DX	25-40	32	32
80486SX	20-25	32	32
80486DX	25-100	32	32
Pentium	60-133	32	64

A PC's overall processing capability is directly related to the internal clock speed and the width of the data paths. For example, a 33 MHz 80386DX is roughly 10 times more powerful than the original 8088 microprocessor. The 80286 (or 286 for short) microprocessor suffices for many home applications. However, we need at least the processing power of the 80386DX for graphics used in desktop publishing or computer-aided design (CAD) applications. PC applications are often limited not by the speed of the hardware, but by the speed of the human sitting at the keyboard. Don't be discouraged if you don't have the latest chip. The 386 and 486 chips, while not as fast and powerful as the Pentium, are adequate for most applications. Because software continues to make use of faster and more powerful processing capabilities, we recommend that newly purchased systems contain the most advanced hardware the user can afford.

Primary Storage (RAM)

Primary storage is a temporary holding location for both software and the data to be processed. Once software is loaded into primary storage, the programmed instructions can be executed by the CPU. The software tells the CPU the location of the data and the processing steps. The amount of primary storage on PCs typically ranges from 640KB to 8MB. A **kilobyte (KB),** roughly equivalent to one thousand characters, is 1024 bytes. A **megabyte (MB)** is one million bytes. Only the 8088 chip is severely limited in memory capacity, with memory limited to 1MB.

Because these storage locations are accessible by DOS in any order, primary storage is called **RAM** (**Random Access Memory**). Software and all data must reside in RAM to be processed. Data contained in storage locations remains there until new values replace it, or until the electricity is turned off. Most RAM chips lose their stored value when power is lost. Thus, primary storage is considered temporary. To permanently save data, you must record it on a **secondary storage device** such as a magnetic disk.

PC users should realize the potential damage that static electricity can do to sensitive electronic circuits. The amount of static electricity that you sometimes feel when you touch a doorknob is much greater than the static electricity needed to damage a microprocessor or RAM chip. You can minimize the potential for static electricity damage by using a static mat to discharge static electricity. Static strips can be mounted below the spacebar on keyboards for the same purpose.

Input/Output Devices

Input/output devices are the means by which you enter data into the computer (input) or view previously entered data (output). The five most common input/output devices are: keyboard, monitor, printer, mouse, and modem.

The Keyboard

The **keyboard** on a PC is an input device similar to a typewriter keyboard, but with additional keys. IBM PC and IBM-compatible keyboards typically have at least 101 keys. The placement of these keys varies among manufacturers. It is important to understand these keys before working with DOS. Figure 1.3 shows the four major areas of the extended keyboard.

Figure 1.3
Typical Extended Keyboard

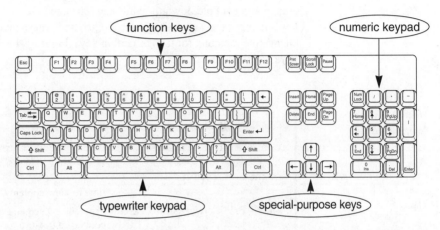

Earlier keyboards have a set of 10 special keys, called **function keys**. These keys, labeled F1 through F10, are located on the left side of the keyboard. Today's extended keyboards have 12 or more function keys located on the top row. Function keys are "programmable" in that they serve different functions depending on how each software program defines their use. This text generally refers to a function key using the key name, such as the F1 key or the F6 key; occasionally, it is shown inside brackets, such as <F1> or <F6>.

The **numeric keypad** is a group of 17 keys, including keys numbered 0–9, located to the right of the keyboard. When the Num Lock key is on, you can use the keypad to enter numbers. The Num Lock key is a toggle key, one that acts as a switch. Press it once to switch it on; press it again to turn it off. The light on the Num Lock key indicates it is toggled on for numeric input. (Another example of a toggle key is the Caps Lock key, which shifts all lowercase alphabetic characters (a–z) to uppercase (A–Z) when switched on. It only affects alphabetic characters.)

You can also enter numbers by pressing the numeric keys located on the top row of the **typewriter keypad**, located just below the function keys. Hold the Shift key down to enter uppercase alphabetic letters.

Extended keyboards (see Figure 1.3) have **special-purpose keys** that can be used to position the cursor on the screen. For example, pressing the left arrow key once moves the cursor back (or left) one position. The **cursor** is a special character, usually an underline character, which identifies a location on the computer screen where the next action or entry of data will occur.

Some keys are pressed in combination with other keys to enter the desired results. Dual-purpose keys have two characters, an upper and a lower character, shown on each key. To enter the upper symbol on a dual-purpose key in the typewriter area, you must hold down the Shift key. Thus, to enter a $, hold down the Shift key and press the 4 key. The Control (Ctrl) and Alternate (Alt) keys can also change the meaning (or use) of certain keys. Figure 1.4 lists some combination keys and their functions.

Figure 1.4
Combination Keys

COMBINATION KEYS	FUNCTION
Control + Break (Ctrl-Brk)	Cancel (break) the execution of a command or operation.
Control + S (Ctrl-S)	Momentarily stop screen display to allow time to view contents.
Shift + PrintScreen (Shift-PrtSc)	Print current screen contents; must be connected to a printer. (On some keyboards, it is not necessary to press the Shift key.)

As you enter commands or data from a keyboard, you can use the Backspace key, normally shown as a large left-facing arrow (←) to back up and erase unwanted characters. The **Backspace key** erases one character at a time to the left of the current cursor position each time you press the key.

Once a command is completely keyed, it is available to be executed, or entered, by pressing the Enter key. The **Enter key** is located just to the right of the alphabetic keys. On most keyboards it is shown as a bent left-facing arrow (↵). Figure 1.5 summarizes the keyboard keys.

Figure 1.5
Summary of
Keyboard Keys

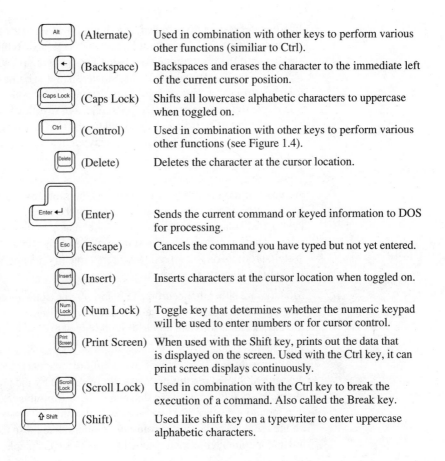

(Alternate)   Used in combination with other keys to perform various other functions (similiar to Ctrl).

(Backspace)   Backspaces and erases the character to the immediate left of the current cursor position.

(Caps Lock)   Shifts all lowercase alphabetic characters to uppercase when toggled on.

(Control)   Used in combination with other keys to perform various other functions (see Figure 1.4).

(Delete)   Deletes the character at the cursor location.

(Enter)   Sends the current command or keyed information to DOS for processing.

(Escape)   Cancels the command you have typed but not yet entered.

(Insert)   Inserts characters at the cursor location when toggled on.

(Num Lock)   Toggle key that determines whether the numeric keypad will be used to enter numbers or for cursor control.

(Print Screen)   When used with the Shift key, prints out the data that is displayed on the screen. Used with the Ctrl key, it can print screen displays continuously.

(Scroll Lock)   Used in combination with the Ctrl key to break the execution of a command. Also called the Break key.

(Shift)   Used like shift key on a typewriter to enter uppercase alphabetic characters.

Because modern keyboards are electronic and not mechanical, a very light touch activates the keys. If you continue to hold down a key, the keyboard will repeat that keystroke until you release that key. This repeating key feature may cause problems for you until you get used to it. It is best to strike most keys with a quick tap.

In computer terminology, a **buffer** is a holding area that can temporarily store computer characters. For example, the keyboard has a buffer that retains keystrokes until the program you are using has "caught up" with you. When you use a program that processes input data slower than it is being keyed, the buffer can save keystrokes for processing. If you happen to lay your textbook on the keyboard, pressing keys repeatedly, the buffer will overflow and the computer will begin beeping to alert you of the problem. Buffers, used to improve the efficiency of processing disk files, are discussed in a later chapter.

The Monitor

Another important input/output device is the **monitor** (screen), which allows the personal computer to communicate with the user. Keystrokes entered at the keyboard display on the screen to provide visual verification. When the computer communicates with you, it normally displays data, error messages, and system prompts on the screen. Monitors typically display 80 characters on a line and 25 lines on the screen.

Monitors are either monochrome or color. Monochrome monitors are limited to a single color such as amber, green, or white. Most users prefer color monitors to take full advantage of software applications designed to display many different colors.

The sharpness and clarity of images on the screen are directly related to the **screen resolution**. The higher the resolution, the clearer the image becomes on the screen. Screen resolution is usually measured by the number of **picture elements (pixels)** on a screen that can be lit to form images. The lowest resolution monitors display 320 pixels horizontally and 200 pixels vertically (320×200) on the screen. The highest resolution monitors, like those used by engineers and artists for computer graphics, may have 1024×1024 pixels, or more.

Control units, called **graphics adapters**, enable the monitor to communicate with the CPU. The graphics system, the monitor and its graphics adapter, is referred to collectively as CGA, EGA, VGA, SVGA, and so on.

CGA stands for Color Graphics Adapter. The first control unit for color monitors, it had relatively low resolution and very limited number of colors. **EGA** (Enhanced Graphics Adapter) offered better resolution and more colors than does CGA. **VGA** (Video Graphics Array) was introduced by IBM to provide superior colors, high-resolution graphics, and very readable text. One of the latest graphic adapters, **SVGA** (Super VGA), offers very high resolution and many outstanding colors. Graphics adapters are designed to be downward-compatible. Thus, a VGA system can run software designed for a CGA or an EGA system, but not software designed for an SVGA system.

The Printer

Printers for PCs are classified as either letter quality or draft quality (dot matrix). Most **letter-quality printers** create each character by striking a fully formed image of a character against an inked ribbon and paper. They print documents that look as if they were created by a typewriter. **Draft-quality printers** use a dot matrix technique that creates a pattern of dots to represent each character or image. They produce images of lesser quality but are sufficient for most applications. Many dot matrix printers produce near letter-quality output by reprinting each character, adding dots to fill the image with a denser pattern of dots. Printing additional dots increases printing time. However, **dot matrix printers** are usually faster and less expensive than letter-quality printers. In addition, dot matrix printers are more flexible in that they can print many patterns, including graphics.

Alternatives to inked ribbon printers include ink jet and laser printers. These nonimpact printers are very quiet. **Ink jet printers** spray ink on a page to create high-quality characters. A relatively inexpensive type of ink jet printer, called a bubble jet printer, may be used at home to create letter-quality documents. The **laser printer** is the fastest and most expensive type of printer. It uses a process similar to that of copy machines. Laser printers produce letter-quality output, including graphic images, and allow for many different sizes and styles of characters. Laser printers are used extensively in many business and desktop publishing applications.

The Mouse

Most PCs include a **mouse** as a pointing device. As you move the mouse across a flat surface, it relays information to the computer that moves the cursor (usually shown as an arrow) in the same direction. You press (or click) a button on the mouse (similar to pressing the Enter key) to inform the computer that you have selected the desired spot on the screen. Special software, called a mouse driver, is required to use a mouse to control the cursor. This software is included when you purchase the mouse hardware.

The Modem

To communicate with other computers via telephone lines, you need at least two items: a modem (at each end) and communication software. A **modem** converts the computer's digital signals to the analog signals (tones) used by telephones, and vice versa. A modem at the other end converts an analog tone back to a digital character, such as 01000001. The speed with which the modem can send and receive data is called its **baud rate**. The higher the baud rate, the less time it takes to send and receive data. Common baud rates are 1200 and 2400, but data can be sent over phone lines at rates as high as 9600 baud. If you divide the baud rate by 10, you can approximate the data transmission rate in characters per second. Thus, 2400 baud is approximately 240 characters per second.

Communication software is readily available to enable you to use your modem effectively. The function of communication software is to assist you in setting up the various communication parameters required to let your computer talk to another computer. Communication parameters include baud rate, information for encoding/decoding the bit patterns, and method of error detection and correction during transmission.

The I/O Interface

Any **input/output (I/O) device** attached to a CPU needs a control unit to allow it to interact with the CPU. Control units make the proper translations between I/O devices and the CPU. Each control unit, called an **interface board**, consists of a sturdy card containing electronic chips. These easily removed cards plug directly into slots on the CPU's system board.

The **system board** is the large printed circuit board that contains your microprocessor and primary storage RAM chips. The number of **expansion slots** available depends on the system board. System boards often have expansion slots for a monitor (video display adapter), two serial devices (such as a mouse and a modem), a parallel device (such as a printer), and slots for disk drives. Each slot is connected to a common communication link called a **data bus**. The bigger the data bus, the faster data can be processed inside the CPU. The bus sizes vary on a PC from 8-bit to 64-bit paths (see Figure 1.2).

Slots for a variety of serial and parallel devices are called **ports**. Data goes through a **serial port** via a single wire, one bit at a time. Most serial ports use an industry standard called the RS-232 serial interface. Because each character requires 8 bits, serial transmission is relatively slow. Faster speeds are obtained with a **parallel port**, which use eight parallel wires to send data 8 bits at a time.

SCSI (pronounced "scuzzy") is a relatively new type of serial port. It is both fast and versatile. **SCSI ports** are used to add a variety of devices, including large hard drives, tape systems for backup, and CD-ROM drives.

Secondary Storage

When you create data on a computer or write programs, nothing is saved permanently in RAM, the computer's primary storage area. RAM is not large enough to store many files containing data and/or programs. **Secondary storage** facilities store large amounts of data permanently. The cost per bit of secondary storage is far less than primary storage. PCs support several types of secondary storage devices, including removable floppy disks and fixed hard disks.

Floppy Disks

Floppy disks are the most common medium for secondary storage and come in various sizes (Figure 1.6). Initially, the most common size for PCs was the 5¼-inch disk, which held 360KB (roughly 360,000 characters) of data. Disk drives record data on circular positions around the surface of the disk, called tracks. A 360KB floppy disk has 40 tracks per side for storing data. High-density 5¼-inch disks have a higher quality magnetic coating on the surface of the disk; they can fit 80 tracks on a side, storing 1,200,000 bytes (1.2MB) of data. Today the most common floppy disk is the 3½-inch disk. These disks come in a hard plastic case and use improved technology to record data as follows: 720KB (low density), 1.44MB (high density), or 2.88MB (extended density) of data.

Figure 1.6
Floppy Disks

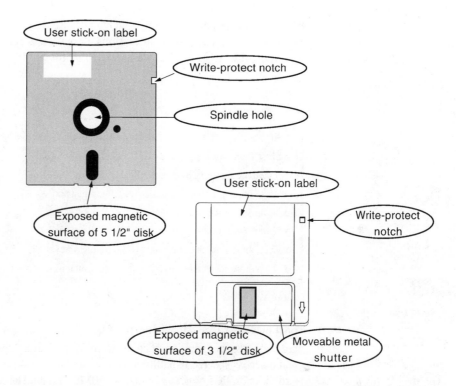

To protect a 5¼-inch disk from being changed, place a sticky tab (or piece of tape that comes packaged with the disks) over the write-protect notch. This notch is located on the left side as you insert the disk into a horizontally mounted drive.

To protect a 3½-inch disk, move the small sliding tile in the write-protect notch so that it *does not* cover the hole. You can write to a 3½-inch disk only if this hole is open. Note: high-density 3½-inch disks have an extra hole that identifies the density type to the drive. It is located opposite the write-protect notch (not shown in Figure 1.6) and is always open.

When you insert a 5¼-inch floppy disk into a floppy disk drive and close the latch, the disk is secured by two clamps that close on the large center hole of the disk. If the latch is not securely closed, an error message will inform you that the disk cannot be accessed. When data is read from or written to a 5¼-inch disk, a motor connected to the clamps spins the disk inside its protective jacket. A small red light on the disk drive indicates that the drive is spinning. *Do not remove the disk when the red light is on.*

Floppy disks are not completely reliable because they can be easily damaged. However, if you take proper precautions, floppy disks can serve you faithfully for a long time. Figure 1.7 contains some helpful and important tips for using floppy disks.

Figure 1.7
Proper Care of
Floppy Disks

- Always store floppies in their protective covers when not in use.
- Store them vertically to lessen the chances of warping.
- Shade them from direct sunlight and intense heat.
- Write on any attached labels with felt-tip pens only.
- Never touch the recording surface of a floppy disk.
- Never bend, fold, or otherwise crimp a floppy disk.
- Keep disks free of contaminants, including smoke.
- Keep them away from magnetic sources, such as electric motors.

Hard Disks

Hard disks are also called fixed disks because they are not removable. When the hard disk drive is operating, it spins much faster than a floppy disk, allowing for greater access speeds. In addition, you do not have to continually swap disks. Hard disks on PCs typically hold 40–450MB of data. Hard disks store data using a much higher density, allowing for many more tracks per side than floppy disks. This is because the disk surfaces are rigid metal platters in a sealed environment, free from contamination. A 40MB hard disk, for example, can store more data than one hundred 360KB floppy disks. Figure 1.8 shows a hard disk with a cut-away view of the platters.

Figure 1.8
Hard Disk

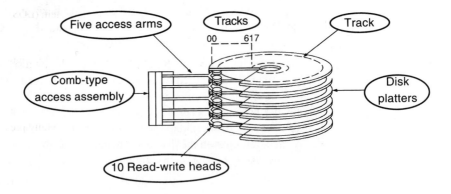

It is not practical for personal computers to have only a hard disk drive. Floppy disks are used for transferring data and programs from one computer to another and for backup. Applications generally require at least one hard disk drive and one floppy disk drive. Figure 1.9 identifies the major differences between floppy and hard disks.

Figure 1.9
Comparison of Floppy
Disks and Hard Disks

	FLOPPY DISK	HARD DISK
Portability	Removable	Fixed
Processing Speed	Very slow	Much faster
Storage Capacity	Relatively small	Very large
Reliability	Easily damaged	More secure

SOFTWARE

To control and operate the hardware, a computer system must also have **software**. Figure 1.10 outlines the various classifications of software.

Figure 1.10
PC Software

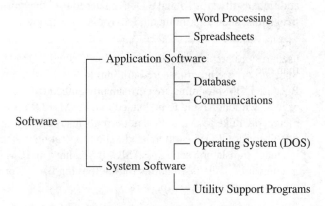

Application Software

Application software is a set of programmed instructions written for a specific purpose, such as word processing or inventory. Many prewritten programs are available at a reasonable cost. An abundance of application software has been written for PCs, including the following general categories:

- *Word processing programs* to create and modify documents.
- *Electronic spreadsheet programs* to manipulate numeric data.

- *Database programs* to keep track of things, such as customers.
- *Communication programs* to "talk" to other computers.
- *Application programs* for accounting, budgeting, payroll, and so on.

System Software

Your computer system needs an **operating system** to act as a translator between the application programs and the hardware. Application programs can run on a computer only after the operating system has been loaded. This process, called "booting the system," is covered later. The operating system lets you control the computer's operations and manage files. Most operating systems let you use the computer in an interactive or a batch mode. With **interactive processing**, the user enters a command for the computer to execute immediately. When the computer finishes that command, the user issues another command. **Batch processing** occurs after a user creates and saves a file of commands. Once the batch file is created, the user can enter a single command that tells the system to execute all the commands in the file one after another. This text covers both methods of processing.

System software normally includes an operating system and a set of supporting utility programs. For example, the operating system this text covers is DOS (Disk Operating System). It is normally included when you purchase a PC. Even with the power and many capabilities of DOS, many users found the need for additional software. To make DOS easier to use, they turned to **utility support programs,** such as Automenu, PC-Tools, or Windows.

The last topic to discuss before delving into DOS is a hybrid type of hardware used to store preprogrammed instructions, called **ROM (Read-Only Memory)**. Special-purpose programs are built into ROM chips during manufacturing. Because ROM programs are permanently embedded into computer memory, they execute without having to be loaded into RAM. ROM is a form of permanent memory. Unlike RAM, it does not lose its instructions when the power is turned off. Therefore, ROM is often used to hold operating system startup programs and language translators, such as BASIC. If you have an IBM PC (not an IBM clone or compatible), the instructions for interpreting BASIC programs are contained on a proprietary ROM chip.

When you turn on your computer system, a ROM chip first tests the hardware for problems. Then it loads a portion of DOS from the default disk drive. In the future, more software (including DOS) will become available on inexpensive ROM chips. Laptops and other portable PCs may contain both the operating system and several common application programs in ROM. This will make them lighter and faster, and reduce the amount of disk storage required.

Chapter 1

REVIEW
QUESTIONS

1. What are the four major hardware parts of a PC?
2. What is the major difference between primary storage and secondary storage?
3. What is the major difference between RAM and ROM?
4. What is the purpose of a clock rate in a microprocessor?
5. What is the potential danger of static electricity?
6. What is the purpose of function keys?
7. What is a toggle key?
8. Give two examples of toggle keys found on the keyboard.
9. Give two examples of combination keys found on the keyboard.
10. What happens when you press the Backspace key?
11. Describe the repeating key concept.
12. What term defines the sharpness and clarity of images on the display screen?
13. What is the significance of having more bits in an addressable unit of RAM?
14. What are some advantages that dot matrix printers have over letter-quality printers?
15. What are the two most common forms of secondary storage on PCs?
16. What are the major differences between hard disks and floppy disks?
17. What is the difference between application software and system software?
18. What is the purpose of utility support programs?
19. What is the difference between batch and interactive processing?
20. What is the function of a data bus?

Chapter 1

EXERCISES

1. Using what you learned in this chapter, list the components for the computers in your lab. This may require asking some questions because not all of the information may be obvious.
2. Match the seven components (labeled A–G) in Figure 1.11 on the next page to the component names provided below it. As in the previous exercise, this may require some additional information. However, you can make some good educated guesses from the material covered in this chapter.

Figure 1.11
Personal Computer and
Data Bus

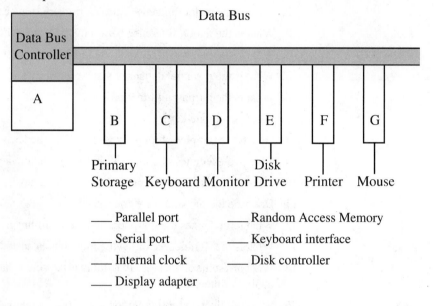

____ Parallel port   ____ Random Access Memory

____ Serial port   ____ Keyboard interface

____ Internal clock   ____ Disk controller

____ Display adapter

3. Using information obtained from computer magazines, newspapers, or people who sell PCs, find the current price range for each of the following hardware items:

	Without Controller	With Controller
Super VGA Monitor	_____	_____
Laser Printer	_____	N/A
Mouse (with software)	_____	N/A
Internal Modem	_____	N/A
Floppy Disk Drive (3½")	_____	_____
Hard Disk (120MB)	_____	_____

INTRODUCTION TO DOS CONCEPTS

BASIC DOS FUNCTIONS

    Control Input/Output Operations

    Interpret and Execute Commands

    Manage Files

SAVING FILES WITH DOS

WORKING WITH HARD DISKS

UNDERSTANDING DIRECTORIES AND SUBDIRECTORIES

BOOTING DOS

    Booting from a Floppy Disk

    Entering the Date and Time

    Booting from a Hard Disk

INTRODUCTION TO DOS CONCEPTS

The primary goal of Chapter 2 is to teach you the basic functions of DOS for command processing and file management. By the end of this chapter, you will understand how files are saved on disk, why we use subdirectories with hard disks, and how to load (boot) DOS.

An **operating system**, such as DOS, is a set of programs that is an integral part of all computer systems. Without an operating system, you could not use your computer. For example, suppose you wanted to use a word processing program to create a term paper. The operating system allows you to load and execute programs. In addition, application programs use the operating system to save and retrieve disk files. Your computer's operating system (DOS) provides all these capabilities, and more.

DOS is a necessary translator between hardware and application programs; it coordinates and controls all activities of the computer (Figure 2.1). DOS contains a group of commands and programs that let you interact directly with the computer. For example, it provides an easy way to copy data from one disk to another, allowing you to make backup copies of important data. Understanding DOS will help you run your application programs and will make you a more effective user.

Figure 2.1

The Role of an Operating System

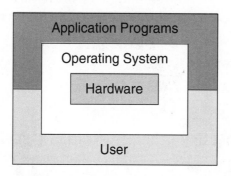

This text discusses a specific disk operating system called MS-DOS (Microsoft DOS). Another disk operating system, PC-DOS (Personal Computer DOS), is written by IBM. Both systems are used with IBM and IBM-compatible PCs. IBM and Microsoft have worked closely together to ensure that PC-DOS and MS-DOS are very similar. Thus, we refer to either operating system simply as DOS.

(Note: MS-DOS was used to create the figures and examples in this text.)

BASIC DOS FUNCTIONS

DOS has three major functions to help you use your computer. It controls the input and output operations of your computer, it interprets and executes commands entered from your keyboard, and it saves files on disk and lets you manage your files effectively.

Control Input/Output Operations

All application programs share the same input and output requirements. They all accept data from the keyboard, display data on the monitor, store data temporarily in main memory, store data permanently on disk, and retrieve data from disks. It requires many instructions to coordinate and control activities on a PC. Without an operating system, each application program would have to duplicate these instructions.

Three "hidden" files typically reside on an MS-DOS system disk: MSDOS.SYS, IO.SYS, and DBLSPACE.BIN. These system files provide the input/output instructions required by DOS and by application programs. **Hidden files** do not appear on your screen when you list the files on your DOS disk. **MSDOS.SYS** provides all the support functions necessary for application programs to run on your system. These functions are primarily related to disk operations. **IO.SYS** contains additions to the basic I/O system routines built into your system on ROM chips. IO.SYS holds the device drivers (instructions) DOS uses to operate other devices attached to your system, such as the screen, printer, and keyboard. **DBLSPACE.BIN** lets DOS compress data stored on your hard disk, effectively doubling the storage space. In PC-DOS, the hidden system files are named differently, but perform the same functions.

Interpret and Execute Commands

The command processor part of DOS interprets and executes the commands you enter, as well as commands from application programs. Without an operating system, you would have no effective way to communicate with the hardware and direct its activities. In MS-DOS (and PC-DOS) these functions are provided by the **COMMAND.COM** file.

Manage Files

As a user, you are heavily involved with the file management role of DOS. For example, before you can save files you must prepare (format) the disk to record files. Once a disk is formatted, you may save, rename, copy, or delete files. DOS provides a series of commands to allow users and application programs to manage the multitude of disk files created over time. Most of this text is devoted to file management commands.

SAVING FILES WITH DOS

A **file** is a set of related information items saved as a single group and given a filename. Because the information saved consists of either program instructions or data, a file is either an executable **program file** or a **data file**. For example, a word processing program is a program file and a document you create with it is a data file. When you save a file with a filename that already exists on the disk, the contents of the existing file are deleted and replaced by the information in the new file. If you save a file with a new name, it is automatically added to the disk.

Saving files on disk is a function of all operating systems. The files you create and use in RAM are temporary and become permanent only when you save them on disk. When you turn off the computer or otherwise lose power, the contents of RAM (program and data files) are erased. However, files saved on disk can be recalled (retrieved) when needed. Application programs routinely direct DOS to save files. Although it may seem like a simple process, many steps are required to save files. The following overview explains this process.

1. IBM and IBM-compatible floppy disk drives are double-sided, meaning data is stored on both sides of the disk. Disk speed increases when you access both sides of a disk before moving to another track. The areas on a formatted disk used to record data are made up of **sectors** and **tracks** (Figure 2.2). Identical sectors on the top and bottom surface of a disk combine to form a cluster. A **cluster** is the smallest addressable location that can save data on a disk. The term **allocation unit** also refers to a cluster. Each sector on a 360KB disk contains 512 bytes, so the cluster size is 1024 bytes. Cluster sizes vary depending on the disk drive used and the number of read/write heads per track. Large cluster sizes improve performance of disk access when files are large. When files are smaller than a cluster, the unused space in the cluster cannot be used by another file.

Figure 2.2
Partial Diagram of a Floppy Disk

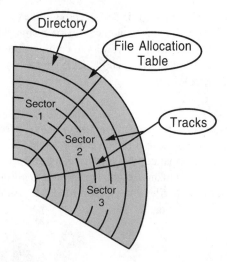

2. When you issue a save command from an application program or directly from DOS, the operating system finds an unused area (unallocated clusters) to store the file. Because DOS uses whatever clusters it can find to store the file, the clusters are not always adjoining. Files written in noncontiguous (separated) clusters are called **fragmented files**. The additional head movement caused by fragmentation slows the time it takes to process these files. Figure 2.3 shows how file fragmentation occurs.

Figure 2.3
File Fragmentation

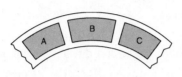
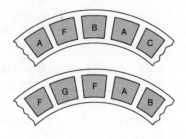
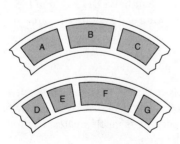

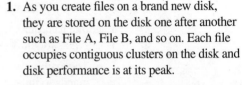

1. As you create files on a brand new disk, they are stored on the disk one after another such as File A, File B, and so on. Each file occupies contiguous clusters on the disk and disk performance is at its peak.

2. Whenever you delete a file, a "hole" is left where the file was stored. To save a large file, DOS may have to use multiple non-adjoining holes, causing the file to be fragmented. Pieces of your files can be scattered all over your disk. The time required to access fragmented files can be many times slower than nonfragmented files, depending on the extent of fragmentation.

3. One way to eliminate fragmentation of files is to copy all your files to a newly formatted disk. A better way is to use the DEFRAG command, a disk optimization program covered in Chapter 8. It rearranges all files on a disk into contiguous clusters.

3. DOS keeps track of which clusters contain data and which ones are free to store data. This area of the disk is called the **File Allocation Table (FAT)**. When DOS saves a file, the FAT is updated with the cluster information used to store (and retrieve) the file. If a file is fragmented, the entries in the FAT form a "chain" that DOS follows whenever it needs to access the file.

4. DOS then updates the **directory** on the disk with important information about the file. The directory, along with the FAT, is stored in a reserved area of track zero on each disk. The file information stored on the disk's directory is as follows:

- filename and filename extension

- file size (in bytes)

- date and time of creation or last change

- starting cluster location in the FAT

- status of file attributes

Each file has four specific qualities called **attributes**. The status of each attribute is stored as file information on the disk directory as follows:

- The **archive** attribute is used by BACKUP, XCOPY, and other DOS commands to indicate that files have been saved (archived) to another location. When files are created (or subsequently modified), DOS sets the archive attribute on, showing that it has not been saved.

- The **read-only** attribute is used to protect a file from being accidentally changed or deleted. When the read-only attribute is set on (with the ATTRIB command), you may read the file, but you cannot change or delete the file without first setting the attribute off.

- The **hidden** attribute tells DOS to bypass displaying the filename on a normal directory listing.

- The **system** attribute identifies a DOS system file. These files contain data relating to your hardware and system software.

WORKING WITH HARD DISKS

As noted in Chapter 1, hard disks have two significant advantages over floppy disks: the speed at which data transfers is significantly faster, and the amount of data that can be stored per disk is much greater. The following two operational items relate to hard disk systems.

1. The first consideration is the need for a *good power supply* that does not allow loss of electrical power. A temporary power loss may cause the disk's read/write heads to "crash" on the surface of the disk, causing permanent damage. To ensure continuous power for hard disk systems, a standby power supply is recommended. A continuous supply of electricity protects the data on the disk and the disk drive. For a cost of about $250, buying a good power backup system for business computers is a wise investment.

2. Another consideration is the need for *periodic backup* of the data stored on your hard disk. Backup means to copy important files to floppy disks. Although backup is equally important for data stored on floppy disks, hard

disk users often overlook this important operation. Get into the habit of backing up your hard disk regularly. You will be glad you did the day you turn on your computer and hear a noise like a spoon in a blender.

UNDERSTANDING DIRECTORIES AND SUBDIRECTORIES

Because large amounts of data are stored on a hard disk, users find it necessary to divide the total space into uniquely named work areas on the disk. Each area, called a **subdirectory**, is used to store a specific group of files. Subdirectories let you organize and classify files by application. You can establish subdirectories on floppy disks, but using directories is essential with hard disks. Hard disks have too many files to keep track of without organizing them into logical subdirectories. The term *directory* is often used to represent a subdirectory. Therefore, we will use the terms *directory* and *subdirectory* interchangeably.

One way to visualize the concept of directories is to compare a single 40MB hard disk to a set of one hundred floppy disks. Conceptually, each directory can represent a single floppy disk, without the size limitations. Like floppy disks, each directory can be used for a given application, such as word processing, spreadsheet, accounting, and so on. You can change to a specific directory, just as you insert another floppy disk.

Another way to think of directories is to relate them to how data is organized in a filing cabinet. Each drawer could be thought of as a directory. Large hanging folders in each drawer could represent dozens of lower-level directories within each of the main directories. Additionally, individual file folders in the hanging folders could be even lower-level directories.

You can organize and control hundreds of files on a hard disk by adopting a tree-structured file directory system. The **root directory** branches into directories. Each directory can branch into further directories. The tree-like hierarchy is similar to a family tree or business organization chart. Figure 2.4 shows an example of a tree-structured directory on a hard disk.

Figure 2.4
Sample Hierarchy
of Directories

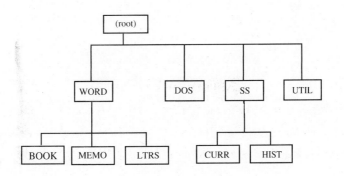

In this typical tree structure, the root directory is subdivided into four directories: one for word processing, one for DOS, one for spreadsheets, and one for utility programs. The word processing directory (WORD) is further subdivided into three directories: books, memos, and letters. DOS navigates through this structure by starting at the root. It travels through the required branches to get to the desired directory.

Floppy disk files are often organized manually by saving selected groups of files on a disk and identifying each disk with a label. Hard disk directories provide a big advantage in that they allow you to organize all the files "electronically." Files may be added quickly and new directories created as needed.

BOOTING DOS

Before any computer can be used, its operating system must be loaded into RAM. There is not enough room in RAM to store all of DOS, so only a small portion of DOS is loaded at a time. Loading is called **booting the system**.

There are two ways to boot DOS. One is with a **cold boot**, when the computer is off prior to the boot process and the hardware is cold. A **warm boot** is used when the computer is already on, but needs to be booted again.

The major difference between the two ways of booting the system is how the boot process begins. For a cold boot, you turn on the computer to boot DOS. For a warm boot, you enter a sequence of three keys simultaneously: the Control key, the Alternate key, and the Delete key (Ctrl-Alt-Del). Most PCs have a reset button that can be pressed to do a warm boot.

Because the computer is an electronic device, do a warm boot whenever possible. The sudden surge of electricity that occurs when the power is turned on can sometimes damage sensitive electronic chips. One good reason for a cold boot, however, when sharing a computer with others, is that a cold boot erases RAM, which may help to prevent the spread of virus programs from previous users.

Booting from a Floppy Disk

To do a cold boot of DOS from a floppy disk, insert the disk containing DOS in Drive A. Drive A is usually the top or leftmost drive in PCs with two floppy disk drives. To initiate the cold boot, turn on the power to both the monitor and the CPU. The boot process involves the six steps shown in Figure 2.5 on the next page and described below.

1. The PC begins by executing a small startup program stored in a ROM chip to run some predetermined diagnostic tests. These tests include checking the computer's RAM and keyboard to make sure they are functional. If there are any problems, the program displays an error message on your screen. For example, if your computer beeps and displays "KEYBOARD ERROR PRESS F1 TO RESUME," your keyboard may be disconnected. If this happens, turn off the system, plug in the keyboard, and do another cold boot.

2. After the computer passes the diagnostic checks, the program in ROM loads the hidden DOS files from your DOS disk in Drive A. These hidden files remain in RAM while the power stays on.

3. At this point, DOS looks for an optional **CONFIG.SYS** file used to specify the different ways your system can be configured, or customized. The CONFIG.SYS file is covered in Chapter 11.

4. Then, DOS loads a file called COMMAND.COM into RAM from Drive A. The **COMMAND.COM** file contains many of the DOS commands you will use, including instructions to load and process all commands entered.

5. DOS looks for another file on Drive A called **AUTOEXEC.BAT**. If found, DOS executes any additional instructions it contains. Using an AUTOEXEC.BAT file, explained in Chapter 10, can simplify the booting process by executing the same set of commands each time you boot DOS.

6. If there is no AUTOEXEC.BAT file, DOS waits for you to enter the correct date and time. DOS has its own system clock to keep track of the time while the computer is on. After obtaining the date and time, DOS displays its version number and prompts you to enter a command.

Figure 2.5
The Boot Process

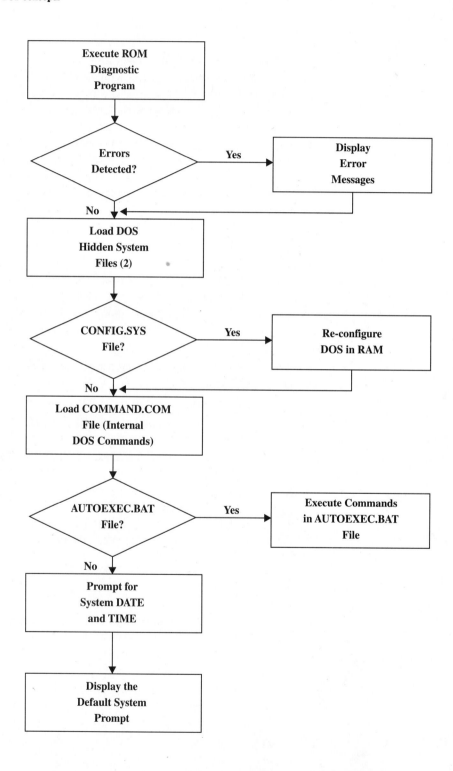

Entering the Date and Time

The system date is entered using month, day, and year in the form of mm-dd-yy. You can use either a slash (/), a hyphen (-), or a period (.) to separate the date entries. As with all operating systems, when you enter a command or some data, like the date or time, you must press the Enter key to let the system know you are finished keying. Figure 2.6 shows you how the screen might look after you entered a date of December 25, 1993, and a time of 2:35 p.m. For illustrative purposes, the data entered displays with bold characters.

Figure 2.6

Screen Display after Booting DOS 6

```
Starting MS-DOS...
Current date is Sat 07-24-1993
Enter new date (mm-dd-yy): 12-25-93
Current time is 10:03:21.72a
Enter new time: 2.35p
Microsoft(R) MS-DOS(R) Version 6.20
            (C)Copyright Microsoft Corp 1981-1993.

A:\>
```

Enter the system time using hours, minutes, seconds, and hundredths of seconds in the form of hh:mm:ss:xx. The use of minutes (mm), seconds (ss), and hundredths of seconds (xx) is optional. You may enter time using the 24-hour system (military time) or the 12-hour system. To use a 12-hour system, key in the appropriate letter (a or p) after the time. Use a colon (:) or a period (.) to separate time entries. Thus, you may enter **13.45, 13:45, 1.45p** or **1:45p** to indicate 1:45 in the afternoon.

After DOS is booted, you are prompted to enter a command. When booting from a floppy disk, the initial **system prompt** is A:\>, where A represents the disk drive containing DOS. The underline character following the system prompt is the cursor. Your next keystroke will be placed (echoed) on the screen at the cursor location.

To change the date after DOS is booted, enter **DATE** (or **date**) at the system prompt and press the Enter key. Use either uppercase or lowercase letters for DOS commands. DOS displays the current date and asks for a new date.

The format of the new date is the same as with the boot process (mm-dd-yy). When entering the date, you do not have to enter leading zeros. For example, enter **07** or **7** for July. You do not have to enter the century. Thus, you can enter **94** to represent 1994.

To change the time, enter **TIME** (or **time**) and press the Enter key. Change the time using the same syntax as before. For example, you can enter **20:15** or **8:15p** to represent 8:15 p.m. DATE and TIME are two DOS commands covered in Chapter 5.

Booting from a Hard Disk

The boot process is almost identical for hard disk systems with two exceptions:

1. If there is no floppy disk in Drive A, most PC systems are designed to look for the files needed to boot the system on the hard disk, which is Drive C. Make sure there is no floppy disk in Drive A, or that Drive A is unlatched when booting from a hard disk. Whenever Drive C is used to boot the system, C:\> (or something similar) becomes the initial system prompt.

2. Most hard disk systems have a battery operated clock-calendar that keeps track of the date and time when the power is off. Typically, a program in ROM contains instructions that automatically set the system clock (date and time) from this battery-operated clock.

Chapter 2

REVIEW QUESTIONS

1. What are the main purposes of an operating system?
2. What does "booting the system" mean?
3. Why are hidden files on a DOS disk?
4. Why do you think DOS writes on both sides of a floppy disk before moving to another track?
5. Why should you boot your system with the correct date and time?
6. What is the function of the File Allocation Table (FAT)?
7. What is the difference between a warm boot and a cold boot?
8. How do you tell DOS to do a warm boot?
9. What is the purpose of the COMMAND.COM file?
10. When are commands in an AUTOEXEC.BAT file executed?
11. How can you change the system date after the system is booted?
12. How would you enter a time of 2:35 p.m. when prompted to do so?
13. What is the difference between MS-DOS and PC-DOS?

14. What is the difference between a program file and a data file?

15. Describe a cluster (allocation unit).

16. How do disk files become fragmented?

17. What is the purpose of a disk's directory?

18. What is a file attribute?

19. How can you protect a disk file from being accidentally deleted?

20. Describe a subdirectory.

Chapter 2

FLOPPY DISK LAB EXERCISE

This exercise assumes that the system is already turned on. If it is not on, do a cold boot before you continue. This exercise is for computers with two floppy disk drives. The DOS disk should be in Drive A. If you are working with a hard disk system with a single floppy disk, skip ahead to the hard disk exercise.

Do a warm boot from a floppy disk:

1. With the DOS disk in Drive A, use Ctrl-Alt-Del to boot the system.

2. Enter the date in mm-dd-yy format (for example, 9-15-94).

3. Enter the time in hh:mm format (for example, 13:07 or 1.07p).

4. Press the Enter key to cause the computer to act on your data.

This completes the Chapter 2 floppy disk lab exercise. Please remove your DOS disk before you leave the computer.

Chapter 2

HARD DISK LAB EXERCISE

The DOS commands should already be loaded on your hard disk (C:). They should be stored in a separate and specific directory on the hard disk. If your computer is off, do a cold boot before proceeding.

Do a warm boot from a hard disk:

1. Remove any floppy disk from Drive A and press Ctrl-Alt-Del to warm boot the system.

2. If your computer does not have a battery-operated clock that automatically sets the system clock when you boot the system, you will have to enter the date in mm-dd-yy format (for example, 9-15-94). Then, enter the time in hh:mm format (for example, 8:07 or 2:15p). Don't forget to press the Enter key to cause the computer to act on your data.

This completes the Chapter 2 hard disk lab exercise.

INTRODUCTION TO DOS COMMANDS

FUNDAMENTAL DOS COMMAND CONCEPTS

Default Disk Drive

Standard Device Names

File Naming Conventions

DOS Directory Listings

Wildcard Characters

Internal and External DOS Commands

Versions of DOS

FORMATTING DISKS WITH DOS

The Formatting Process

HELP Command

FORMAT Command

INTRODUCTION TO DOS COMMANDS

The objective of Chapter 3 is to provide a general understanding of DOS commands. Because DOS is consistent in applying basic concepts, it is easier to learn how to use DOS commands once you understand the fundamentals. This chapter will introduce you to the syntax used to enter DOS commands, using the HELP and FORMAT commands as examples. The HELP command lets you obtain on-line help concerning the use and syntax of any DOS command. The FORMAT command is used to prepare disks for recording data.

FUNDAMENTAL DOS COMMAND CONCEPTS

Before learning specific DOS commands, it is helpful to understand the following concepts applicable to all DOS commands.

- The default disk drive
- Standard device names used by DOS
- The need for effective file naming conventions
- DOS directory listings
- The use of wildcard characters
- Internal and external DOS commands
- Versions of DOS

Default Disk Drive

Most computer systems have at least two disk drives. Applications on floppy disk systems often require that a program disk is in one drive and your data disk in another. If your computer has only one floppy disk drive, it will likely also have a hard disk. A hard disk can easily store both application programs and data. However, you still need a floppy disk drive to load files from floppy disks to the hard disk or to make backup copies of your hard disk files.

When running DOS, the system needs to know what disk drive is the target of the commands you enter. DOS employs the **default drive** concept that lets you specify which of the disk drives is to be the default. Whenever you enter a command and do not specify a disk drive, DOS substitutes the default drive for the missing one(s) in the command. By understanding how DOS uses the default drive concept, you can save keystrokes when entering commands. *Remember, you only need to designate a disk drive if it is other than the default drive.* Initially, however, it is best if you learn to enter the disk drive to help you understand how DOS operates.

To identify the different disk drives, DOS uses a coding scheme consisting of letters. The letters A and B are used for floppy drives, and C through Z are used for hard disk drives. The drive used to boot the system is the initial default disk drive. You can change the default to become another drive at any time. If you boot DOS from a floppy disk and get the A:\> prompt, the A refers to the default disk drive. If you boot from a hard disk, the default disk is Drive C and the prompt will read C:\>. This is the way DOS reminds you which drive is the current default drive. The remaining characters (:\>) are symbols DOS uses to help identify the system prompt; they will be discussed later.

To change the default drive, you must enter a new disk drive letter followed by a colon. For example, to change the default drive to B, type B: and press the Enter key.

Once the new drive letter is entered, DOS reads the new drive, changes the default drive, and displays the new system prompt. You will get an error message if the new drive specified does not contain a formatted disk.

Standard Device Names

DOS reserves certain names to represent system devices. For example, the reserved word **PRN** refers to the printer. Printer designations can be used to copy a file to your printer for a hard copy listing. Because reserved words have specific meanings to DOS, you should never use them to name a file. Figure 3.1 contains a listing of some of these device names.

Figure 3.1
Reserved DOS Device Names

DEVICE NAME	DESCRIPTION
AUX	Auxiliary serial port
CLOCK$	System clock
COMn	Serial communications port (n = 1 to 4)
CON	Console (keyboard)
LPTn	Parallel printer port (n = 1 to 3)
PRN	Printer (attached to LPT1)

File Naming Conventions

DOS uses the **full filename** to tell it where to search for a file. The full filename consists of four parts: disk drive designator, path, filename, and filename extension. The optional parts show in brackets as follows:

```
[d:][path]filename[.ext]
```

The first part of the full filename, **[d:]**, specifies the disk drive. To specify a drive, enter the drive letter followed by a colon. If you omit the drive, DOS substitutes the default disk drive.

The next part, **[path]**, is the location of the subdirectory containing the file. For example, all DOS commands are normally stored in a single subdirectory on a hard disk. If you omit the path, DOS will default to the current subdirectory.

Because floppy disks are small and rarely divided into subdirectories, a path is rarely used with floppy disk files.

Only the **filename** is always required when naming a file. Filenames can be from one to eight characters in length. Filenames consist of uppercase or lowercase alphabetic letters, numeric digits, and a few special characters such as hyphens and underscores. You should avoid using any of the special characters, other than the hyphen (-), which helps make filenames more readable. Spaces and punctuation such as periods, commas, colons, or semicolons are invalid characters in a filename.

Always use meaningful filenames to further classify the type of data contained in each file. A great deal of information can be coded into your filenames. For example, a set of documents on the new bottling plant could be named BOTTLE1.DOC, BOTTLE2.DOC, and so on. If the memo dates were critical, the filenames could be BOTmmdd.DOC, where mm represents the month created and dd is the day. Later you will see how wildcard characters are used to select a specific group of files. When you display a sorted file directory, the memos list together in chronological sequence. As the number of files grows, the benefits of care and foresight in creating filenames become more significant.

The final part of the full filename is an optional extension. The **extension** uses the same set of characters valid for filenames, but it is limited to three characters. Filename extensions, such as DOC, must be preceded by a period (.DOC). Filename extensions help you to identify the category of each file. When an extension is used within a filename, it becomes a permanent part of the full name. Except for executable program files (Figure 3.2), the extension must be included when requesting DOS to access the file. All executable files (programs) in DOS are named with either a COM, an EXE, or a BAT extension. They are executed by entering the filename without the extension. For example, the program to format a disk, FORMAT.COM, is executed by entering the command FORMAT. You should abide by the standard extensions already established and commonly used. Application programs, which also assign filenames, often use the standard extensions shown in Figure 3.2.

**Figure 3.2
Standard Filename
Extensions**

Executable files (executed by entering just the filename with no extension):

BAT — Batch file (file containing executable commands)

COM — Machine language program file (limited in size to 64KB)

EXE — Machine language program file (larger than COM files)

Text files (not executable, but can be displayed on the screen):

BAK — Backup text file

BAS — BASIC program file (needs compiling first)

DAT — Data file

DBF — dBase file

DOC — Documentation file

HLP — Help file (contains help instructions)

INI — Initialization file (like DOSSHELL.INI)

PRN — Printer file (can be modified prior to printing)

SYS — System ASCII file (like CONFIG.SYS)

TXT — Text file

Other files (not executable and not in a form that can be displayed):

DEF — Program definition (setup) file

FON — Font file

GIF — GIF graphics image file

OVL — Overlay file (used by large programs)

PIF — Program information file (memory allocation in Windows)

SYS — System binary file like (ANSI.SYS)

TIF — TIFF graphics image file

WKI — Lotus 1-2-3 worksheet file

WPG — WordPerfect graphics file

DOS Directory Listings

When DOS displays a **directory listing** on your screen, DOS provides more than just the filenames. The file size in bytes and the date stamp is also displayed for each file listed. The **date stamp** is the date and time that each file was last written to the disk. To help you manage files on your disk, you should enter the correct date and time each time DOS is booted. Figure 3.3 shows you a partial directory listing of a DOS 6 disk. The filename extensions are displayed in columnar form to make them easy to find. Directory <DIR> entries are explained in Chapter 7. Note: Version 6.2 of DOS added commas in the display of numbers greater than 999.

Figure 3.3
**Partial MS-DOS
Disk Directory**

```
        Volume in drive C is PENWORTH
        Volume Serial Number is 1B74-6F10
        Directory of C:\DOS

        .               <DIR>        01-01-80  10:57p
        ..              <DIR>        01-01-80  10:57p
        ANSI     SYS         9,065 09-30-93   6:20a
        ATTRIB   EXE        11,208 09-30-93   6:20a
        AUTOEXEC UMB           340 11-20-93   4:15p
        CHKDSK   EXE        12,241 09-30-93   6:20a
        CHKLIST  MS          2,025 10-17-93   6:29p
        CHKSTATE SYS        41,600 09-30-93   6:20a
        CHOICE   COM         1,754 09-30-93   6:20a
        COMMAND  COM        54,619 09-30-93   6:20a
        CONFIG   UMB           302 11-20-93   1:56p
        DBLSPACE BIN        64,246 09-30-93   6:20a
        DBLSPACE EXE       177,034 09-30-93   6:20a
        DBLSPACE HLP        80,724 09-30-93   6:20a
        DBLSPACE INF         2,620 09-30-93   6:20a
        DBLSPACE SYS        22,502 09-30-93   6:20a
        DBLWIN   HLP         8,597 09-30-93   6:20a
        DEBUG    EXE        15,718 09-30-93   6:20a
        DEFRAG   EXE        79,177 09-30-93   6:20a
        Press any key to continue . . .
```

Wildcard Characters

Wildcard characters represent different filename characters in DOS commands, like jokers in a card game. DOS uses two wildcard characters: the asterisk (*), representing a group of one or more characters, and the question mark (?), representing only a single character.

The best way to understand wildcard characters is through examples. The **DIR** command (covered in Chapter 5) displays the names of files stored on a disk. By using wildcard characters, the DIR command can selectively display a group of filenames. Thus, to display a directory listing of all the files on Drive A that begin with the characters LTR and that have an extension of DOC, you can enter **DIR A:LTR*.DOC**. In this example, the asterisk represents any group of characters, so that files named LTRSMITH.DOC, LTR4.DOC, and LTRBILL3.DOC would be included on the directory listing.

To identify all the files on Drive A that have a single character following LTR, enter: **DIR A:LTR?.DOC**. In this example, the files named LTR1.DOC, LTR2.DOC, and LTRX.DOC would be included. Wildcard characters may also be used with filename extensions as follows:

DIR A:TEXT.*	(list all files on Drive A with a filename of TEXT and having any extension)
DIR A:LTR*.*	(list any filename on Drive A starting with LTR and having any extension)

Try some examples using your DOS disk. If DOS is booted, enter the following commands at the system prompt, pressing the Enter key after each command:

DIR	(lists all files on the default disk or directory)
DIR *.EXE	(lists only files with an EXE extension)

DIR S*.*} (lists only files that begin with an S and have any extension)

DOS automatically translates all command keystrokes to uppercase characters, so you may enter DOS commands using either uppercase or lowercase letters. Furthermore, you can use a combination of both cases. Thus, the commands **Dir**, **dir**, and **DIR** are identical in DOS. To help you remember this feature, many examples in this book use both uppercase and lowercase characters.

Internal and External DOS Commands

A DOS command must be copied into RAM from disk before it can be executed. In addition, there is not enough room for all DOS commands to be in RAM at once. For these reasons, commands are classified into two types, internal and external. **Internal commands** are frequently used and/or relatively small DOS commands loaded into RAM when the system is booted. The DIR command is an example of an internal command.

External commands reside on the DOS disk. They must be copied into RAM each time they are executed from a floppy disk or a hard disk. Most of the filenames shown in Figure 3.3 with EXE or COM extensions are external DOS commands. Other files shown in the figure are primarily system files used by DOS.

Versions of DOS

Major releases of DOS often accompany a major improvement in hardware design. The first version of DOS (Version 1) appeared in 1981 along with the IBM PC. It was severely limited and is now obsolete. DOS 2 included hard disk capability, a necessity for business applications. DOS 3 added networking capability, better file management commands, and support for 3½-inch disks. DOS 4 provided a DOS shell, support for hard disks exceeding 32 megabytes, and allowed for expanded memory beyond 640KB. DOS 5 added improved memory management, a task switcher, a better DOS shell, support for 2.88MB floppy disks, and a command to "undelete" files. DOS 6 added the capability to defragment disks, compress files stored on disk, and detect and eliminate computer viruses on your system. It also provided for better memory management and file protection. Versions of DOS are backward-compatible. Typically, programs designed for one version of DOS execute on all newer versions of DOS as well.

FORMATTING DISKS WITH DOS

Addressable areas (clusters) must be defined before files are saved on a disk. When you purchase a new disk, it is a generic disk. A disk can be used with different PCs, using different operating systems. Even with the same operating system, data is recorded on different types of disks differently. Figure 3.4 shows five different types of floppy disks.

Figure 3.4
Floppy Disk Organization
(Based on Disk Capacity)

	TOTAL DISK CAPACITY				
	360KB	720KB	1.2MB	1.44MB	2.88MB
Disk size	5¼"	3½"	5¼"	3½"	3½"
Density type	low	low	high	high	extended
Sectors/track	9	9	15	18	36
Tracks/side	40	80	80	80	80
Bytes/cluster (allocation unit)	1024	1024	512	512	1024
Number of disks required to copy 10MB of data	29	15	9	8	4

The Formatting Process

Each blank disk (including a new hard disk) must be prepared to record data according to the requirements of DOS and the type of disk. This process, called **formatting**, includes the following:

1. DOS creates addressable areas of the disk called **allocation units** (or clusters). Because each disk drive and operating system has its own addressing scheme, this activity is mandatory before saving files. For example, each of the 80 tracks on one side of a 3½-inch (1.44MB) floppy disk is divided into 18 sectors, giving a total of 1440 sectors per side. Each sector holds 512 bytes of data. Depending on the capacity of a particular disk, the size of an allocation unit might be one sector, two sectors, or more.

2. DOS then checks every sector on the new disk for damage. Sectors not acceptable for storing data are marked by DOS. These bad sectors are never used.

3. DOS creates a disk directory and a File Allocation Table (FAT) on track zero of each disk. DOS uses the directory to keep track of file information. The status of sectors is recorded in the FAT. The format process also updates track zero with a "boot record," to permanently identify the type of disk (e.g., 1.44MB).

4. When you format a disk, DOS displays the status of your disk, including the number of bad sectors found. It's a good idea to replace floppy disks containing bad sectors. The cost of losing data is much higher than the cost of a new floppy disk.

HELP Command

Before we look at specific commands, like the FORMAT command, let's learn about the help facility in DOS. If you are stuck trying to remember what DOS command to use, the **HELP** command may provide the information you need to jog your memory. When you enter HELP at the system prompt, DOS displays the Main DOS Help screen, as shown in Figure 3.5. You should use this command as your doorway to on-line help. It replaces the need for a printed DOS reference manual.

Figure 3.5
First HELP Screen

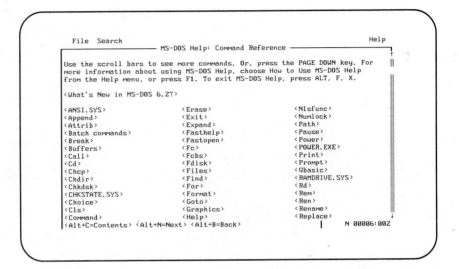

```
     File   Search                                                    Help
                     ──── MS-DOS Help: Command Reference ────
     Use the scroll bars to see more commands. Or, press the PAGE DOWN key. For
     more information about using MS-DOS Help, choose How to Use MS-DOS Help
     from the Help menu, or press F1. To exit MS-DOS Help, press ALT, F, X.

     <What's New in MS-DOS 6.2?>

     <ANSI.SYS>              <Erase>                <Nlsfunc>
     <Append>               <Exit>                 <Numlock>
     <Attrib>               <Expand>               <Path>
     <Batch commands>       <Fasthelp>             <Pause>
     <Break>                <Fastopen>             <Power>
     <Buffers>              <Fc>                   <POWER.EXE>
     <Call>                 <Fcbs>                 <Print>
     <Cd>                   <Fdisk>                <Prompt>
     <Chcp>                 <Files>                <Qbasic>
     <Chdir>                <Find>                 <RAMDRIVE.SYS>
     <Chkdsk>               <For>                  <Rd>
     <CHKSTATE.SYS>         <Format>               <Rem>
     <Choice>               <Goto>                 <Ren>
     <Cls>                  <Graphics>             <Rename>
     <Command>              <Help>                 <Replace>
     <Alt+C=Contents> <Alt+N=Next> <Alt+B=Back>              N 00006:002
```

To view information about any command or DOS subject, use the Up and Down arrow keys to highlight a command, and then press the Enter key. The Tab key moves to the next column. If you have a mouse, "click on" the command name by pointing to the name and pressing the left mouse button.

When selected, most commands have supplemental information (Notes and Examples) that are viewed on request. These hypertext links are surrounded with green pointers on a color monitor. If you request *Notes*, DOS displays general information, tips, and warnings for the command. The *Examples* option shows you how to use the command's syntax.

Once you know what command you want to use, you can view the syntax of a command by entering the command name along with the HELP command. For example, suppose you wanted help with the FORMAT command. Figure 3.6 shows what is displayed when you enter the command **HELP FORMAT**. Experiment using the HELP command, first with just HELP and then with specific commands that interest you. To exit HELP, press Alt-F to use the File pull-down menu. Then, press X to select the option marked eXit.

Figure 3.6
Syntax of the FORMAT
Command Using HELP

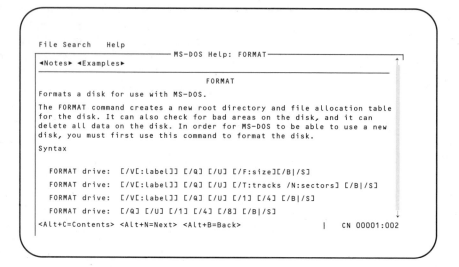

```
 File Search    Help
                        ─── MS-DOS Help: FORMAT ───
 ◄Notes► ◄Examples►

                             FORMAT
 Formats a disk for use with MS-DOS.

 The FORMAT command creates a new root directory and file allocation table
 for the disk. It can also check for bad areas on the disk, and it can
 delete all data on the disk. In order for MS-DOS to be able to use a new
 disk, you must first use this command to format the disk.
 Syntax

   FORMAT drive:  [/V[:label]] [/Q] [/U] [/F:size][/B|/S]

   FORMAT drive:  [/V[:label]] [/Q] [/U] [/T:tracks /N:sectors] [/B|/S]

   FORMAT drive:  [/V[:label]] [/Q] [/U] [/1] [/4] [/B|/S]

   FORMAT drive:  [/Q] [/U] [/1] [/4] [/8] [/B|/S]
 <Alt+C=Contents> <Alt+N=Next> <Alt+B=Back>            |   CN 00001:002
```

The syntax of DOS commands used in this text will be much easier to follow
than that in Figure 3.6. To simplify the process of understanding and using DOS,
only the most common command parameters and options are included in this
text. Additional information is obtained with the HELP command.

FORMAT Command   Syntax: `[d:][path]FORMAT d: [/F:size] [/S] [/U]`

The **FORMAT** command prepares a disk in the designated drive to record data
acceptable to DOS. All disks must be formatted before they can be used by DOS.
During the format process of a 360KB disk, two write heads prepare 40 tracks
(0–39) on each side for recording data. On other floppy disks, 80 tracks (0–79)
are prepared. FORMAT examines each disk for defective sectors, making a note
on the FAT of the bad sectors. The FORMAT command prompts you to enter a
volume label to give your disk a name. Besides establishing a disk directory and
FAT, DOS randomly generates a disk serial number. This unique identifier does
not change unless the disk is formatted again.

To make a disk bootable, use the /S option. It formats the disk and copies the
hidden system files, such as IO.SYS and MSDOS.SYS, and the
COMMAND.COM file from a DOS disk. The slash (/) identifies a command
option to DOS. The term *switch* also represents a command option.

Another useful option is the /F option that specifies the size of the floppy disk to
format. Use this option to format a 720KB disk in a 1.44MB floppy disk drive
(i.e., /F:720). Due to the technical limitations of a low-density drive, you cannot
format a 1.44MB disk in a 720KB disk drive. Figure 3.7 shows a screen display
of a format operation using the /F option. Refer to your on-line HELP command
for more information about this and other FORMAT options.

Figure 3.7
Screen Display of FORMAT
with /F Option

```
C:\DOS>format b:/s/f:720
Insert new diskette for drive B:
and press ENTER when ready...

Checking existing disk format.
Saving UNFORMAT information.
Verifying 720K
Format complete.
System transferred

Volume label (11 characters, ENTER for none)? dos62

      730,112 bytes total disk space
      199,680 bytes used by system
      530,432 bytes available on disk

        1,024 bytes in each allocation unit.
          518 allocation units available on disk.

Volume Serial Number is 141B-13E4

Format another (Y/N)?n

C:\DOS>
```

FORMAT produces a status report on the screen with the following statistics for the formatted disk: total disk space, sectors marked as defective (if any), space allocated to the system files (when /S is used), the amount of space left for other files, and information about the allocation units.

When you format a disk all existing files are marked as "deleted" by DOS. A special system file is recorded on the formatted disk that makes it possible to "unformat" the disk with the UNFORMAT command. You can use the HELP command to find out more information about UNFORMAT. Of course, it is only possible to restore the disk if the disk has not been written to after formatting. The /U option is used to physically delete all existing files on a disk, making it impossible to unformat. It is quicker to format a disk that has never been formatted by using the /U option because no existing information has to be saved by DOS.

Examples of usage:

A:\> FORMAT b:/s
(format the disk in Drive B so that it contains the system files, making it bootable)

B:\> A:format B:
(format the disk in Drive B, using the FORMAT command on drive A)

A:\> format b: /f:720
(format the disk in Drive B as a 720KB disk)

A:\> FORMAT B:/U/F:360
(format the disk in Drive B as a 360KB disk, deleting all existing files)

Chapter 3

REVIEW
QUESTIONS

1. What is meant by the term *default drive* in DOS?

2. What do the standard device names CON and PRN represent?

3. Define the four parts of the full filename.

4. How is a filename extension identified by DOS?

5. What kind of file would likely have an extension of .SYS?

6. What are some common extensions for text files that are not executable, but may be displayed on the screen?

7. What are some common extensions for executable files?

8. In the command **DIR *.SYS**, what does the "*" represent?

9. Why is it important to name files correctly?

10. What is a date stamp in a disk's directory?

11. How do internal commands differ from external commands in DOS?

12. Give an example of an internal DOS command.

13. Give three examples of external DOS commands.

14. Why is the command **DIR** the same as the command **dir** in DOS?

15. When the command **HELP** is entered, what is displayed on the screen?

16. How can you view the syntax of the CHKDSK command in DOS?

17. What is a bad sector on a disk?

18. What is the purpose of the FORMAT command?

19. Why would you want to use the /S option with FORMAT?

20. What is the purpose of a status report when formatting a disk?

Chapter 3

FLOPPY DISK
LAB
EXERCISE

This exercise assumes that the system is already turned on. If it is not on, do a cold boot before you continue. This exercise is for computers with two floppy disk drives. The DOS disk should be in Drive A. If you are working with a hard disk system with a single floppy disk, skip ahead to the hard disk exercise. Otherwise, format a data disk to contain the DOS system files:

1. Enter **FORMAT B:/S** (remember, you can use lowercase characters).

2. Insert a blank disk in Drive B and press the Enter key.

3. Enter your name as the volume label (up to 11 characters with no special characters) when prompted to do so by DOS. You may use spaces in the label.

4. Enter **N** (or **n**) when prompted to format another disk. Figure 3.7 shows what the screen should look like when you finish formatting a 720KB blank floppy disk.

This completes the Chapter 3 floppy disk lab exercise. Remove your floppy disk(s) before you leave the computer.

Chapter 3

HARD DISK LAB EXERCISE

The DOS commands should already be loaded on your hard disk (C:). They should be stored in a separate subdirectory. For the examples in this book, we will assume that the subdirectory containing the DOS commands is named C:\DOS. If your computer is off, do a cold boot before proceeding.

Use the **DIR** command to view the files on the current directory. If the current directory does not contain your DOS commands, use the CD command to change to the appropriate directory (i.e., CD\DOS). Then format a data disk in Drive A to contain the DOS system files:

1. Enter **FORMAT A:/S** (remember, you can use lowercase characters).

2. Insert a blank disk in Drive A and press the Enter key to continue.

3. Enter your name as the volume label (up to 11 characters with no special characters) when prompted to do so by DOS. You may use spaces in the label.

4. Enter **N** (or **n**) when prompted to format another disk. Figure 3.7 shows what the screen should look similar to when you finish formatting a 720KB blank floppy disk.

This completes the Chapter 3 hard disk lab exercise. Remove your data disk before you leave the computer.

INTRODUCTION TO THE DOS SHELL

DOS SHELL BASICS

    The Shell Window

    Pull-down Menus

    Dialog Boxes

    Selecting and Choosing

STARTING THE DOS SHELL

USING THE SHELL WITH THE KEYBOARD

USING THE SHELL WITH A MOUSE

CHANGING THE SHELL COLORS

FORMATTING A DISK WITH THE SHELL

RUNNING DOS COMMANDS FROM THE SHELL

EXITING THE DOS SHELL

    Returning with the EXIT Command

    Using the Command Prompt

There has been much discussion as to the merits of using the DOS shell. If you are a new user to DOS, you will likely find the DOS shell a handy feature. Those who are already familiar with entering commands at the system prompt may find it slow by comparison. The primary objective of this chapter is to introduce you to how the shell operates. Later chapters will include additional operations using the shell. After completing the hands-on work in this book, you can form your own opinion about the shell.

The DOS shell is a user-friendly alternative to entering commands at the system prompt. Information displays on the screen in a more visual form. Using a keyboard or a mouse, users simply point to select files and execute commands. The shell's purpose is to simplify the process of entering DOS commands.

DOS SHELL BASICS

The DOS shell uses a "window" approach for displaying information on the screen. The greatest benefit of the window approach is that users don't have to memorize so much. For example, directory listings are displayed to help you locate and select files to be processed. In addition, DOS commands listed in a window can be selected for execution without having to remember how to spell the command. The first screen you see when you use the DOS shell looks similar to Figure 4.1.

**Figure 4.1
The DOS Shell Window
in Text Mode**

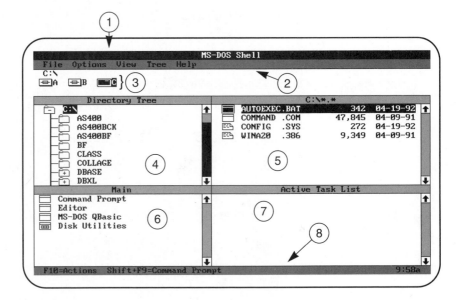

A **window** is a well-defined portion of the screen devoted to providing specific information to the user. A window can list files on a disk or a set of commands to execute. Like windows in a building, a window can be a single pane or it can be subdivided into multiple panes. With the DOS shell, the term *window* normally refers to a given pane, called an *area* or *box*. Some windows are displayed next to each other; others can overlay portions of previous windows.

The Shell Window

The DOS shell window has eight major areas. These areas, noted in Figure 4.1, are as follows:

1. The *Title Bar* tells you that the shell is activated.

2. The *Menu Bar* displays the pull-down menu items that can be selected.

3. The *Drive List* shows you the possible disk drives you can select as the default drive. As Figure 4.1 shows, the current default drive is highlighted (shown darker than the other drive letters). The data displayed in the remaining windows all relates to the selected disk drive.

4. The *Directory Tree* area displays the subdirectories on the default disk drive alphabetically. The root directory is initially highlighted as the current subdirectory. A + or − symbol next to a subdirectory name indicates that it contains additional subdirectories.

5. The *File List* area, to the right of the Directory Tree area, lists the files in the current directory alphabetically. The first file in the directory is always selected and highlighted as the default file.

6. The *Main* program menu area shows you a list of program names installed to run from the shell, including the Command Prompt that lets you execute any DOS command from within the shell.

7. The *Active Task List* area is used for task swapping, covered later. It will not be shown unless the task swapper is activated.

8. The *Status Bar* displays available keystrokes, the current system time, and any system messages.

Pull-down Menus

The window approach gives users a highly visible way to work. Most activities are initiated by using pull-down menus. A **pull-down menu** is a small window superimposed on the DOS shell screen. It lists a set of related actions or commands for a major type of activity. For example, Figure 4.2 contains the pull-down menu for file-oriented commands.

Figure 4.2
File Pull-down Menu

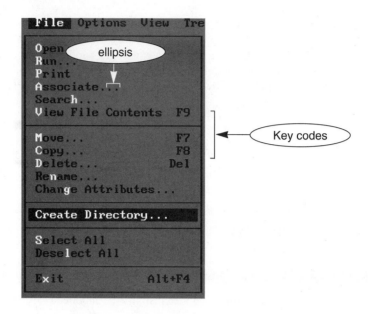

In the File menu in Figure 4.2, some commands have an ellipsis (...) next to their names. An ellipsis shows that the shell will require further information to execute the command. Some commands have a key code next to their name, such as F7 or F8. These keys are "short-cut" keys because they activate a command without your having to first pull down the command menu. Later we will discuss several other ways you can choose commands from a pull-down menu. Shaded commands are not currently available for use.

Dialog Boxes

The DOS shell uses dialog boxes to request information that it needs to carry out a task. **Dialog boxes** are like pull-down menus in that they overlay existing windows when displayed. Figure 4.3 contains two dialog boxes used by the DOS shell, one to obtain file display options and the other to select a display color scheme.

Figure 4.3
Sample Dialog Boxes

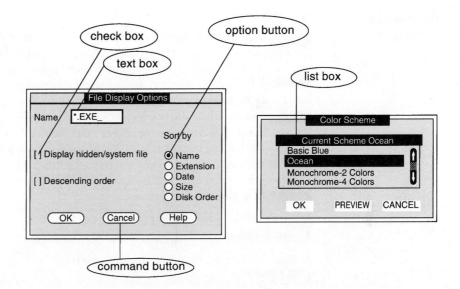

Most dialog boxes allow you to enter information in several ways:

- **Check box**   A set of brackets forming a box containing an X or a blank space; it is changed by selecting the box. You can select as many boxes with an X as you need.

- **List box**   A listing of choices that can be selected. Where permitted, you can select as many items as you need. Selected items become highlighted in the box.

- **Text box**   A place where you can enter text from the keyboard. A row of dots shows where the text is entered.

- **Option button** A listing of options, each with its own input area. You can select only one option at a time. When you select an option, it displays a dot.

- **Command buttons** A set of immediate actions to be carried out based on the information selected in the rest of the box. You can select only one command button (such as OK, Cancel, or Help) to be executed.

Selecting and Choosing

Working with the shell usually involves two related processes, selecting and choosing. First you must **select** a desired file from a window on the screen. To select a file, use the arrow keys to point to (highlight) a file and then press the Enter key. To cancel a selection, simply select (highlight) another filename. Next, you can **choose** some type of action for the highlighted file by activating a pull-down menu. There are two methods to activate a pull-down menu from the keyboard. One way is to press the F10 key and the first letter of the desired activity shown in the menu bar at the top of the screen. Another method is to hold down the Alternate (Alt) key and press the first letter of the desired activity. Suppose you wanted to view the contents of a file. Conceptually, these are the four steps used to view a file:

1. Move to the File List window.

2. Select the file in the list, causing it to become highlighted.

3. Press Alt-F to activate the File pull-down menu.

4. Press V to choose the View option to display the highlighted file.

STARTING THE DOS SHELL

The shell may start automatically, depending on how your system is configured when you booted DOS. Once you see a window displayed like Figure 4.1, the shell is active and ready for use. If the shell was not started automatically on your computer, start it by entering the following command at the system prompt:

```
C:\DOS> DOSSHELL -or- DOSSHELL/G
```

If you have an EGA or VGA monitor, install the shell using the *graphics mode*, rather than the *text mode*. In the graphics mode, graphic images (*icons*) appear in the window next to directory names and filenames. Use **DOSSHELL/G** to load the shell in the graphics mode. Because the mode you choose is recorded in the DOSSHELL.INI file, used by DOS to load the shell, you only have to specify the /G option the first time.

USING THE SHELL WITH THE KEYBOARD

The Tab key moves from one window to another. The Esc key lets you exit from a menu or dialog box. Let's see how we can display the contents of the DOSSHELL.INI file.

1. To select a file, press the Tab key until the File List area is highlighted. The File List area is just to the right of the Directory Tree area, in the center of the screen.

2. Use the arrow keys to highlight the DOSSHELL.INI file. Use the Up arrow or Down arrow keys to scroll a line at a time. If a list is long, you can use the PgUp or PgDn keys to scroll one page at a time.

3. Press Alt-F to activate the File pull-down menu.

4. Press the underlined letter of the desired command. Now, press V (for View) to display the contents of the highlighted file.

5. Press the Esc key to exit displaying the file.

USING THE SHELL WITH A MOUSE

If you have a mouse installed, you should see a mouse pointer on the screen. If the shell was executed in the text mode, it will show as a small, lightly shaded rectangle. In the graphics mode, the mouse pointer displays as an arrow. If you can't locate the mouse pointer on the screen, try moving the mouse.

To *select* an item in a shell window, move the mouse pointer to the desired item and click on the item. The left mouse button is tapped once to click on a selection. To *choose* an action you must "double-click" on a command. Double-clicking is performed by quickly pressing and releasing the left mouse button twice. This is equivalent to clicking on a selection, and then pressing the Enter key. Besides using the mouse to highlight files and actions, you can click on the scroll bars to vertically scroll through the contents of an area, such as a long File List.

To use the menu bar with a mouse, click on an item in the menu bar to display the pull-down menu and then click on the desired command. To cancel a pull-down menu, you may press the Esc key, click on the menu name again, or click anywhere outside the menu area.

CHANGING THE SHELL COLORS

Suppose you want to change the color scheme of the shell as shown in Figure 4.3. The following shows how you can select an item from a list using either the keyboard or a mouse:

KEYBOARD: Press Alt-O to select the Options menu. Choose O (Colors) to see the Color Scheme dialog box. Highlight the desired color using the arrow keys, or press the first letter of a color. To preview the colors use the Tab key to select the Preview command button and press the Enter key. If you wish to skip the preview process, press the Enter key to execute the change. Press the Esc key to cancel an operation.

> MOUSE: Click on Options in the menu bar to display the Options menu. Click on Color Scheme and then on the desired color. Click on the appropriate command button to execute the command.

After the color scheme changes, use what you have learned to change it back to the original colors. Otherwise, the color changes will remain for the next student when you exit the shell.

FORMATTING A DISK WITH THE SHELL

Let's see how the DOS shell is used to execute a command you executed in Chapter 3 using the command line, the FORMAT command. Using either the keyboard or a mouse, do the following steps:

1. Move to the Main program menu area and activate the Disk Utilities submenu.

> KEYBOARD: Each time you press the Tab key, the next window area is selected (highlighted). Press the Tab key until the Main program menu area is selected. Then press the Down arrow key three times to highlight Disk Utilities and press the Enter key.

> MOUSE: Move the mouse pointer to the Disk Utilities entry (not the icon) in the Main program menu area and double-click the left mouse button.

2. Activate the Format program from the Disk Utilities list.

> KEYBOARD: Press the Down arrow key five times (or press F) to highlight Format. Press the Enter key to select.

> MOUSE: Double-click on the Format entry (not the icon).

3. Provide the necessary parameters to execute the Format program.

> KEYBOARD: Enter the appropriate information to format a disk. For example, to format a bootable disk in Drive B, enter **B:/S** in the text box and press the Enter key. If the default disk drive (shown in the text box) is correct, press the Right arrow key to add the /S.

> MOUSE: Enter data using the keyboard as above. Then, press the Enter key, or click on the appropriate command button.

4. Follow system directions to get back to the DOS shell Main menu.

RUNNING DOS COMMANDS FROM THE SHELL

There are several ways to run DOS commands from the shell. You have already seen how to run the Format program from the Disk Utilities submenu. In addition, many DOS commands are included in the set of actions found in the menu bar. Here are two other ways to execute DOS commands:

1. If the command you want to run needs no parameters, you can choose it from the File List area. For example, let's run the CHKDSK command to see the status of the default disk. When CHKDSK is finished, press any key to return to the shell.

KEYBOARD: Use the Tab key and arrow keys to select the DOS directory from the Directory Tree area and press the Enter key. Then, highlight the CHKDSK.EXE command in the File List area and press the Enter key to execute the highlighted command.

MOUSE: Click on the DOS directory in the Directory Tree area. Then double-click on the CHKDSK.EXE command in the File List area.

2. When a DOS command requires additional parameters and is not included in the menu bar, you must exit the shell and then execute the command from the system prompt.

EXITING THE DOS SHELL

One way to exit the DOS shell is to activate the File pull-down menu and then select the Exit option. It is faster to use a short-cut key: press the **F3** key to leave the DOS shell immediately. Both methods will exit the shell permanently.

However, it is often advantageous to exit the shell temporarily. This way, you can return to the shell more quickly, without requiring DOS to reload the shell. To leave the DOS shell temporarily and exit to the system prompt, press **Shift-F9**. To return to the shell, you must use the EXIT command.

Returning with the EXIT Command

The **EXIT** command is an internal DOS command that lets you return to a program (including the DOS shell) that you left temporarily. Many application programs let you "shell out" to the system prompt to execute DOS commands. This feature is especially common with word processing and spreadsheet programs. Entering **EXIT** at the DOS prompt returns you to the application program.

A word of caution is necessary, however. *If you temporarily exit from the shell, or any application program, you must return with the EXIT command.* If you left the shell using the Shift-F9 key and then entered **DOSSHELL** at the system prompt, there would be two copies of the shell loaded in memory. Because this results in lots of problems, keep track of how you exited the shell.

Using the Command Prompt

Another way of exiting the shell temporarily and executing DOS commands is through the Command Prompt entry in the Main program menu. Once this entry is selected, you can execute as many DOS commands as you like before returning to the shell with the EXIT command. To see how this works, do the following to get on-line help about the CHKDSK command.

KEYBOARD: Use the Tab key to select the Main program menu. If Disk Utilities is currently displayed in this area (from a prior operation), select Main to display the Main program menu. Press the Enter key to execute the highlighted item, Command Prompt. After entering **HELP CHKDSK** at the system prompt, remember to enter **EXIT** to return to the shell.

MOUSE: Click on the Main program menu. If Disk Utilities is currently displayed in this area (from a previous operation), click on Main to display the Main program menu. Double-click on the Command Prompt entry. After entering **HELP CHKDSK** at the system prompt, remember to enter **EXIT** to return to the shell.

Potential Problems Using the DOS Shell

From the Options menu, you can choose Select Across Directories, which lets you select files in more than one directory at a time. We recommend you *do not enable this feature*. Because DOS displays only the filenames in the current directory, you can't see all the filenames you selected. This could lead to inadvertently deleting identically named files from different directories.

Whenever you exit from the DOS shell after making a change to the way it operates (such as changing the screen colors), DOS updates a system file (DOSSHELL.INI) with those changes. DOS uses this system file to tell it how to load and execute the DOS shell.

Don't turn off the computer whenever you have temporarily left the shell and DOS is waiting for an EXIT command to return to the shell. Each time you leave the shell, DOS creates a temporary disk file to help it remember how to return to the same place in the shell. When it returns to the shell, DOS deletes the temporary file. If you power off before DOS has a chance to delete these temporary files, they will occupy space on your disk needlessly.

Chapter 4

REVIEW QUESTIONS

1. What is the major reason for using the DOS shell?

2. What is a benefit of using a "window" approach with DOS?

3. Describe a pull-down menu.

4. What files are displayed in the File List at any given time?

5. Where is the status bar displayed when using the DOS shell?

6. What does an ellipsis (...) indicate on a pull-down menu?

7. What is the "short-cut" key to view the contents of a selected file?

8. What is the purpose of a dialog box?

9. What are the differences between a check box and an option button in a DOS shell dialog box?

10. What is a text box?

11. Explain how "selecting" differs from "choosing" when using the DOS shell.

12. How does the text mode differ from the graphics mode?

13. What is the function of the Tab key in the shell?

14. What is the function of the Esc key in the shell?

15. What is the function of the PgUp and PgDn keys in the shell?

16. What is the function of the F10 key in the shell? Why would you choose not to use it?

17. Describe how a mouse is used to select an entry from a pull-down menu that is not currently displayed.

18. List three different ways to execute DOS commands using the shell.

19. How do you exit from the DOS shell permanently?

20. How do you exit from the shell temporarily and then return?

Chapter 4

LAB EXERCISES

If the DOS shell is not already active, enter the following command at the system prompt: **DOSSHELL** or **DOSSHELL/G**

1. This first exercise using the shell shows you how you can view the contents of a disk file. Normally, you will only want to view a "listable" text file, like AUTOEXEC.BAT or CONFIG.SYS. However, you can also view executable command files that include lots of strange-looking characters. Let's look at the MORE.COM file. Because it is an executable file, only the right side of the screen may be readable. Use the PgUp and PgDn keys to browse through the contents of the file. Exit the view operation by pressing the Esc key.

   KEYBOARD: Use the Tab key and arrow keys to select the DOS directory in the Directory Tree. Use the Down arrow key as many times as necessary to highlight the MORE.COM command in the File List. Now press Alt-F to activate the File menu. Choose V to view the selected file.

   MOUSE: Click on the DOS directory in the Directory Tree. Then locate and click on the MORE.COM command in the File List. Click on File in the menu bar and click on View in the File menu to view the highlighted file.

Now apply what you know to view other files on the File List. View some listable files (those with a BAT, BAS, or TXT extension).

2. This exercise lets you display the File List in a different sequence. More than likely the current File List displays in filename sequence. Reorder the list by file size, so that the largest files appear first (in descending order by size).

KEYBOARD: Press Alt-O to select the Options menu. Press F to choose the File Display Options dialog box (shown in Figure 4.3). Press the Tab key twice to get to the Descending order area. Press the spacebar to put an X in the check box. Press the Tab key again to get to the Sort By area and use the Down arrow key to choose Size. Press the Enter key to execute the change.

MOUSE: Click on the Options menu in the menu bar. Then click on File Display Options, followed by Descending order and Size in the dialog box. Click on the OK command button to execute the change.

After you change the order of the file list, use what you have learned to change it back to the way it was before you started this exercise.

3. This exercise shows how you can easily copy files from one drive to another. Begin by making sure the File List area displays the files relating to DOS 6. These will either be on the DOS subdirectory of Drive C or on Drive A, depending on your system. Select any two files to be copied to your data disk as follows:

KEYBOARD: Highlight the first file you want to copy and then press Shift-F8. This lets you select more than one file from the list. Highlight the second file and press the spacebar to add it to the selected list. Select the Copy command from the File pull-down menu and enter the Drive containing your data disk (i.e., A or B). Respond to the system prompts to complete the copy operation.

MOUSE: Click on the first file to be copied from the file list. While holding down the Ctrl key, click on the second file. After releasing the Ctrl key, "drag" the files from the File List area to the appropriate disk drive icon in the Drive List area. To drag a file in the shell, hold down the left mouse button while moving the pointer from any selected file to the desired location. Respond to the system prompts to complete the copy operation.

4. This exercise lets you add a new program item to the Main program list area. You can add virtually any program or DOS command to the program list. Then, you will add the DOS CHKDSK command to view the status of Drive A. Before you begin, make sure the shell displays the Main program menu area similar to Figure 4.1.

KEYBOARD: Tab to Main in the program list area. Then, press Alt-F (File), N (New), and the Enter key (OK) to display the Add Program dialog box. Type **Check Disk in Drive A** in the program title box and press Tab to move to the Commands box. Type **CHKDSK A:** and press Tab to move to the next box. Press the Enter key to bypass remaining entries. To execute this new command, select the title in the Main program list area.

MOUSE: Click on Main in the program list area. Then, click on File, New, and OK to display the Add Program dialog box. Type **Check Disk in Drive A** in the program title box and press Tab to move to the Commands box. Type **CHKDSK A:** and press Tab to move to the next box. Press the Enter key to bypass remaining entries. To execute this new command, double-click on the title in the Main program list area.

5. Bonus exercise (requires application of prior learning):

Using what you learned from this chapter, delete the two DOS files you copied to your data disk in Exercise 3.

This completes the Chapter 4 lab exercises. We will be using the DOS shell throughout the remainder of the text.

INTERNAL COMMANDS

INTERNAL COMMANDS

This chapter covers ten internal DOS commands often used with floppy disk systems. External commands are covered in Chapter 6. The discussion of each command includes the following items:

- The general syntax of the command.
- An explanation of the command parameters.
- Helpful options when using the command.
- Some examples of usage at the system prompt.
- Execution of the command from the DOS shell, if applicable.

In addition to the command name itself, DOS commands may have parameters and options. **Parameters** further define the command. For example, they are required with the COPY command to identify the file(s) to be copied. **Options** are switches that tell DOS how to execute the command. They are normally placed at the end of the command line. Parameters and options that apply primarily to hard disk systems are covered later. Remember, DOS commands, including their parameters and options, may be entered using any combination of uppercase or lowercase characters.

Brackets are used in this text to identify the optional parts of a command. The brackets are not to be entered as part of the command. Command options are preceded by a slash (/). Rarely used options are not covered.

One command option, the /? option, is available for use in all DOS commands. This helpful option provides an on-line explanation for the given command. For example, the command **FORMAT /?** explains the syntax of the FORMAT command, including parameters and options. This is similar to entering HELP FORMAT.

A **delimiter** is a special character, or separator, used to separate parts of a DOS command. DOS uses a variety of delimiters, including spaces, commas, and semicolons. The examples in this text normally use a space as a delimiter.

You can stop the execution of a command before normal completion. For example, you can abort DOS commands while they are running by entering Ctrl-C (or Ctrl-Break). When commands display a large amount of output on the screen, Ctrl-S temporarily suspends the display. Pressing any key continues the display process. When software instructions direct you to "Press any key" this normally refers to any alphabetic (A–Z) key, numeric (0–9) key, or the spacebar. It does not refer to any of the special or control keys, such as Ctrl-C.

Invalid commands are rejected by DOS, resulting in an error message, such as "Bad command or filename." You will see this message if the command cannot be found. When a filename is not on the disk specified, you get a "File not Found" error message. If either of these error messages appear, re-enter the command correctly.

The space between the read/write heads and the surface of the disks is very small. Thus, any movement of the disk drive when the disk is operating can be very destructive. If you try to read a disk and no disk is in the designated drive, or the drive latch is open, you get a "Drive not ready" error message. DOS also displays an error message if:

- track zero on a disk is bad and cannot store the FAT and directory,

- the type of disk is not correct (such as a high-density disk in a low-density drive), or

- you try to read data from a defective disk.

Whenever you get an error message for a disk operation, DOS displays the message: "Abort, Retry, Fail?" If you cannot correct the problem, enter **A** to end (abort) the command that requested the disk operation. If you can correct the problem, such as closing a drive latch, fix the problem and enter **R** to retry the operation. The Fail option lets the disk operation fail, but does not abort the command that requested it. Usually, you should retry the disk operation if it is correctable. Otherwise, abort the command. Appendix B describes 30 additional DOS error messages.

Internal commands are part of the COMMAND.COM file loaded into RAM when DOS is booted. Therefore, you do not need to have a DOS disk in a disk drive when executing an internal command. Internal commands covered alphabetically in this chapter are:

CLS   clears the screen of all data

COPY   makes a copy of a disk file

DATE   displays and/or changes the system date

DEL   deletes a file from disk

DIR   displays filenames from a disk

REN   changes the name of an existing file

TIME   displays and/or changes the system time

TYPE   displays the contents of a disk file

VER   displays the DOS version number

VOL   displays a disk volume label

**CLS (Clear Screen)
Command**

Syntax: CLS

The **CLS** command clears all current characters from the monitor (display screen). It results in a blank screen with the system prompt and a blinking cursor in the upper left corner. There are no parameters or options for this command.

Example of usage:

A:\> CLS
(displays only the system prompt on the screen)

COPY Command

Syntax: COPY [d:]filename[.ext] [d:][filename[.ext]]

where the first filename is the source file and the second filename (optional) is the target file (the new file being created).

The **COPY** command lets you copy disk files to a formatted disk. It can make backup copies of files without destroying existing files. Before DOS Version 6.2, files on the target disk with the same name as the target file were replaced by the contents of the source file without warning. Now, if a duplicate filename already exists, DOS (6.2) asks you if you want to overwrite it.

If you omit the disk device designator (d:), DOS substitutes the default drive. If you omit the optional target filename, the system uses the same filename as the source file. When the target filename is the same as the source file, and you do not specify a different disk drive, COPY is aborted with the following error message:

File cannot be copied onto itself

0 file(s) copied

You can copy a group of files with the COPY command by using wildcard characters in the filenames. For example, to copy all files on the default Drive (A:) with an extension of TXT to Drive B, enter:

A:\> COPY *.TXT B:

If you specify the source file as CON (for CONsole keyboard), the target file contains characters entered from the keyboard. Lines are limited to 127 characters each. You must press the Enter key at the end of each line. DOS uses Ctrl-Z to mark the end of a text file. To stop recording characters and insert the Ctrl-Z character, press the **F6** function key, <F6>, followed by the Enter key. Figure 5.1 shows you what the screen might look like if you used the COPY CON command to create a text file on the default disk drive.

Figure 5.1
**Screen Display of the
COPY CON Command**

```
A:\>COPY CON B:READ.ME
When entering DOS commands, the commands and parameters
must be separated by delimiters.  Delimiters are normally
either spaces or commas.  They can used interchangeably
within any command (i.e., COPY A:OLDFILE,B:).^Z
        1 file(s) copied

A:\>
```

COPY CON is often used to type a small file of text, but it is not appropriate for larger files. DOS provides the EDIT command (covered in Chapter 10) for larger text files. Another DOS command to copy files (XCOPY) is covered in Chapter 6.

Examples of usage:

`A:\> COPY *.* B:`
(copies all files on the default disk, Drive A, to the disk in Drive B, without renaming files)

`A:\> COPY *XYZ.* B:`
(identical to the previous example — characters immediately following the first asterisk are ignored by DOS)

`A:\> copy B:*.DOC`
(copies all files on Drive B with an extension of DOC to the default disk)

`A:\> Copy filea.doc b:*.bak`
(copies FILEA.DOC on Drive A to Drive B, renaming it FILEA.BAK)

`A:\> copy con b:read.me`
(creates a file on Drive B named READ.ME consisting of data entered from console)

`A:\> COPY A:FILE*.DOC B:`
(copies all files on Drive A with a DOC extension and that begin with FILE to Drive B)

```
A:\> COPY FILEA.DOC PRN
```
(copies a text file, FILEA.DOC, to the printer)

```
A:\> copy con prn
```
(uses the keyboard like a typewriter, echoing keystrokes to the printer — the F6 key must be entered at the end of typing)

Using the DOS Shell to Copy Files

If you do not wish to experiment using the DOS shell, you can skip this section. If the DOS shell is not active, enter the DOSSHELL command to install the shell. When the shell is activated, make sure the DOS commands display in the File List area. If they are not displayed, use the keyboard or the mouse to select the DOS directory from the Directory Tree area. Now you are ready to practice using the COPY command.

For this exercise, you will be making a backup copy of the ANSI.SYS file. If it is not in the File List, pick another filename that is included. Do the following steps:

1. First, highlight the file you want to copy (ANSI.SYS) in the File List.

2. Display the File pull-down menu from the menu bar.

3. Select the Copy command from the File menu. The ellipses following the name let you know that additional information is required.

4. Because the "From:" file has previously been selected, you only need to enter the "To:" filename. The cursor shows where you start typing text. If text already exists, any text you type replaces it. Optionally, you can use the Left or Right arrow keys to move the cursor and insert or delete text at that point. For this exercise, type **ANSI.BAK** in the "To:" box.

5. After you type the text, press the Enter key to execute the command. The backup file (ANSI.BAK) will now be included in the File List. If you change your mind, you can press the Esc key (or choose the Cancel command button) to exit any operation.

The File menu on the menu bar cannot be used for all copy operations. To use the COPY CON command, you must temporarily exit to the system prompt. Follow the steps below to create a text file from the keyboard:

1. Select the Command Prompt entry from the Main program menu area.

2. Enter the command **COPY CON READ.ME** at the system prompt.

3. Enter the four lines of text following the COPY CON command in Figure 5.1, *pressing the Enter key after all but the last line.*

4. Press the **F6** function key and the **Enter** key to end the last line.

The new file (READ.ME) is now in the File List. If the list is in name sequence, scroll toward the end of the list to make sure it is there.

In addition to the COPY CON command, the DATE, TIME, VER, and VOL commands (described below) are executed from the system prompt.

DATE Command

Syntax: `DATE [mm-dd-yy]` or `[mm/dd/yy]` or `[mm.dd.yy]`

The **DATE** command changes the system date. Values for day, month, and year are separated by hyphens, slashes, or periods. If you specify a new date on the command line, the system is changed. If you have a battery-operated clock-calendar in your PC, its date might also be changed by the DATE command. When you omit the date parameter, the system displays the current date and prompts you to enter a new date. Press the Enter key if you do not wish to change it. If you enter an invalid date, DOS prompts you to enter a correct date. The valid values for the DATE parameter are as follows:

mm = 1 to 12

dd = 1 to 31 (DOS adjusts the maximum value for each month)

yy = 80 through 99 (or, 1980 through 2099)

Examples of usage:

`A:\> DATE 3/4/94`
(changes the system date to March 4, 1994)

`A:\> date 03-04-94`
(also changes the system date to March 4, 1994)

`A:\> DATE 11.15.1995`
(changes the system date to November 15, 1995)

`A:\> Date`
(displays the current date and prompts you to change it)

DEL (Delete) Command

Syntax: `DEL [d:]filename[.ext] [/P]`

The **DEL** command deletes the specified disk file. If the drive designator is not specified, the default drive is used. You can use wildcard characters in the filename and extension, but do so with care. If you use *.* to specify the file, all files on the designated disk could be deleted. In this case, DOS gives you some measure of protection against eliminating files by mistake; it pauses to ask you if you are sure. If you are currently in another subdirectory, you can delete all files in a subdirectory by specifying just the subdirectory name.

You cannot delete read-only files without first changing the status with the ATTRIB command, discussed in Chapter 6. Also, you cannot delete hidden DOS files. Because the **ERASE** command is identical to the DEL command, you may use either command.

If you use the **/P** option, DOS displays the name of the file to be deleted and prompts you with the message "Delete (Y/N)?" When wildcard characters are used, press Y to confirm the deletion, N to cancel the deletion, or Ctrl-C to cancel the DEL command.

The term *delete* may be a little misleading, because files are not physically erased from a disk. The DEL command flags the file's entry on the disk directory as deleted, allowing other data to be written over the space it occupies. Technically, DOS releases space in the FAT and replaces the first character of the filename in the directory with an ASCII 229 character. This character is often shown as a question mark by programs that let you "undelete" files.

ASCII (pronounced Ask-ee) stands for American Standard Code for Information Interchange. It is the name of a standard coding scheme used for text files that can be viewed on the screen with the TYPE command.

Deleted files can often be retrieved with the UNDELETE command, covered in Chapter 6. However, the MS-DOS reference manual from Microsoft includes this important caution in the discussion of the DEL command:

Once you delete a file from your disk, you may not be able to retrieve it. Although the undelete command can retrieve deleted files, it can do so with certainty only if no other files have been created or changed on the disk. If you accidentally delete a file that you want to keep, stop what you are doing and immediately use the undelete command to retrieve the file.

Examples of usage:

```
A:\> DEL a:memo.txt
```
(deletes file MEMO.TXT from Drive A)

```
A:\> DEL MEMO.TXT
```
(deletes file MEMO.TXT from the default drive)

```
A:\> del *.txt
```
(deletes all files on the default drive with a TXT extension)

```
A:\> DEL B:*.* /P
```
(deletes all files on Drive B, prompting you for confirmation before deleting each file)

```
C:\DOS> DEL \TEMP
```
(deletes all files on the subdirectory C:\TEMP)

**Using the DOS Shell
to Delete Files**

Using what you learned earlier, select the ANSI.BAK file (the backup copy) from the File List. Then choose the Delete command from the File pull-down menu and follow the instructions to delete ANSI.BAK.

**DIR (Directory)
Command**

Syntax: `DIR [d:][filename[.ext]] [/Ax] [/Oy] [/P] [/S] [/W]`

The **DIR** command displays a directory, or listing, of the files on a specified disk. It includes the volume identification, the name of each file, the size in bytes of each file, the date and time each file was last modified, and the amount of free space left on the disk. If you do not designate a disk drive, DOS uses the default drive. If you specify a filename, the directory listing includes only that name. Because the filename can contain wildcard characters, you can limit the directory to a specific group of files.

Use the **/A** option to selectively list files based on file attributes. For example, because hidden files don't normally show on DIR listings, the command DIR B:/AH lists only the hidden files on Drive B. The following attribute values may be substituted for "x" in the DIR command syntax:

A   List files whose archive bits are set on

H   List files that are hidden

R   List files that are read-only

S   List files that are system files

–A   List files whose archive bits are set off

–H   List files that are *not* hidden

–R   List files that are *not* read-only

–S   List files that are *not* system files

You can use the **/O** option to sequentially list directory files in a variety of ways. The sequences (or orders) that may be substituted for "y" in the above syntax are as follows:

D   Order by date (oldest to newest)

E   Order alphabetically by extension (ascending)

N   Order alphabetically by name (ascending)

S   Order by file size (smallest to largest)

–D   Order by date (newest to oldest)

–E   Order alphabetically by extension (descending)

–N   Order alphabetically by name (descending)

–S   Order by file size (largest to smallest)

Many users like to use the **/ON** option to have their files listed in name sequence. The SET DIRCMD command changes the default listing sequence for all directory listings. For example, to change the order of all directory listings to filename sequence, enter the following command:

```
A:\> SET DIRCMD = /ON
```

Use the **/P** option to have the computer pause during the display of the directory when the screen is full. It continues displaying again after you press any key to signal you are ready to continue. Figure 5.2 shows what the screen might look like using the pause option with a directory in ascending sequence by filename. The first two <DIR> entries on the listing are system files used to keep track of directory information on the disk.

Figure 5.2

Screen Display of Sorted DIR with Pause (/P) Option

```
Volume in drive C is PENWORTH
Volume Serial Number is 1B74-6F10
Directory of C:\DOS

.                <DIR>         01-01-80  10:57p
..               <DIR>         01-01-80  10:57p
ANSI     SYS         9,065 09-30-93   6:20a
ATTRIB   EXE        11,208 09-30-93   6:20a
AUTOEXEC UMB           340 11-20-93   4:15p
CHKDSK   EXE        12,241 09-30-93   6:20a
CHKLIST  MS          2,025 10-17-93   6:29p
CHKSTATE SYS        41,600 09-30-93   6:20a
CHOICE   COM         1,754 09-30-93   6:20a
COMMAND  COM        54,619 09-30-93   6:20a
CONFIG   UMB           302 11-20-93   1:56p
DBLSPACE BIN        64,246 09-30-93   6:20a
DBLSPACE EXE       177,034 09-30-93   6:20a
DBLSPACE HLP        80,724 09-30-93   6:20a
DBLSPACE INF         2,620 09-30-93   6:20a
DBLSPACE SYS        22,502 09-30-93   6:20a
DBLWIN   HLP         8,597 09-30-93   6:20a
DEBUG    EXE        15,718 09-30-93   6:20a
DEFRAG   EXE        79,177 09-30-93   6:20a
Press any key to continue . . .
```

Use the **/W** option to display the directory in the "wide" format. With this format, only filenames (and any directory names) display, using five columns across the screen. Figure 5.3 shows what your screen might look like using the /W option.

Figure 5.3

Screen Display of Sorted DIR with Wide (/W) Option

```
Directory of C:\DOS

[.]              [..]             ANSI.SYS         ATTRIB.EXE       AUTOEXEC.UMB
CHKDSK.EXE       CHKLIST.MS       CHKSTATE.SYS     CHOICE.COM       COMMAND.COM
CONFIG.UMB       DBLSPACE.BIN     DBLSPACE.EXE     DBLSPACE.HLP     DBLSPACE.INF
DBLSPACE.SYS     DBLWIN.HLP       DEBUG.EXE        DEFRAG.EXE       DEFRAG.HLP
DELTREE.EXE      DISKCOPY.COM     DOSHELP.HLP      DOSKEY.COM       DOSSHELL.GRB
DOSSHELL.COM     DOSSHELL.VID     DOSSHELL.HLP     DOSSHELL.EXE     DOSSHELL.INI
DOSSWAP.EXE      EDIT.COM         EDIT.HLP         EMM386.EXE       EXPAND.EXE
FASTHELP.EXE     FASTOPEN.EXE     FC.EXE           FDISK.EXE        FIND.EXE
FORMAT.COM       GORILLA.BAS      GRAPHICS.COM     GRAPHICS.PRO     HELP.COM
HELP.HLP         HIMEM.SYS        LABEL.EXE        MEM.EXE          MEMMAKER.EXE
MEMMAKER.HLP     MEMMAKER.INF     MEMMAKER.STS     MODE.COM         MORE.COM
MOVE.EXE         MSAV.EXE         MSAV.HLP         MSAV.INI         MSAVHELP.OVL
MSAVIRUS.LST     MSBACKDB.OVL     MSBACKDR.OVL     MSBACKFB.OVL     MSBACKFR.OVL
MSBACKUP.EXE     MSBACKUP.HLP     MSBACKUP.OVL     MSBCONFG.HLP     MSBCONFG.OVL
MSCDEX.EXE       MSD.COM          MSD.EXE          MSTOOLS.DLL      NIBBLES.BAS
POWER.EXE        PRINT.EXE        QBASIC.EXE       QBASIC.HLP       QBASIC.INI
RAMDRIVE.SYS     REPLACE.EXE      SCANDISK.EXE     SCANDISK.INI     SETVER.EXE
SIZER.EXE        SMARTDRV.EXE     SORT.EXE         SUBST.EXE        SYS.COM
TREE.COM         UNDELETE.EXE     UNFORMAT.COM     VSAFE.COM        XCOPY.EXE
        95 file(s)        3,989,826 bytes
                          2,566,144 bytes free

C:\DOS>
```

The **/S** option is used to obtain directory listings of more than one directory. This option lists entries from the current (or specified) directory, and all of its subdirectories.

Examples of usage:

A:\> Dir
(displays a directory of all files on the default disk drive)

A:\> DIR B: /AH
(displays a directory of all hidden files on Drive B)

A:\> dir a:dog*.*
(displays a directory of Drive A, listing only filenames that begin with DOG)

A:\> dir *.doc/o-d
(displays all DOC files on Drive A in new-to-old sequence by date)
Note: The slash serves as a command delimiter.

A:\> dir /w
(displays filenames on the default drive in the wide format)

A:\> DIR B: /ON/W/P
(displays filenames on Drive B, sequenced by filename, in the wide format, pausing after each screen)

C:\WORD> DIR *.DOC /S/P
(displays all DOC files in the WORD directory and its subdirectories, pausing whenever the screen is full)

**Using the DOS Shell
for Directory Listings**

Files in the File List are displayed in different ways. Using the Options menu in the menu bar, the File Display Options dialog box can be selected. This dialog box lets you include hidden files in the File List. It also lets you choose the desired sequence for displaying the files.

**REN (Rename)
Command**

Syntax: `REN [d:]filename[.ext] filename[.ext]`

The **REN** command changes the name of the file specified in the first parameter to the new name given in the second parameter. Wildcard characters are allowed in either parameter. A drive designator is not allowed in the second parameter. REN will not work if the new name already exists on the disk. REN lets you make disguised copies of important files. For example, a spreadsheet file called BUDGET.WK1 can be changed to WORK.EXE. A longer and less common spelling of the REN command is RENAME.

Examples of usage:

`A:\> REN b:ltr1.doc ltr1.bak`
(renames LTR1.DOC on Drive B to LTR1.BAK)

`A:\> ren Ltr1.doc ltr1.bak`
(renames LTR1.DOC on Drive A to LTR1.BAK)

`A:\> rename ltr1.doc *.bak`
(renames LTR1.DOC on Drive A to LTR1.BAK)

`A:\> REN *.TXT *.DOC`
(renames all files with a TXT extension to a DOC extension)

**Using the DOS Shell
to Rename Files**

To rename a file, you must select the filename in the File List. Then, use the File pull-down menu to choose the Rename command. Follow the directions to change the name of the file you created previously, TESTFILE.TXT, to NEWNAME.TXT.

TIME Command

Syntax: `TIME [hh:[mm[:ss]]] [A|P]`

The **TIME** command changes the system time. If your PC has a battery-operated clock-calendar, the TIME command might automatically update its clock as well. You should keep the correct date and time on the system because it is included with the directory information of each file you save. If you omit all parameters, DOS displays the current system time and prompts you to change it. To leave the time unchanged, press the Enter key. If you enter an invalid time, the system prompts you to enter a new time.

The **A|P** parameter specifies a.m. or p.m. for the 12-hour time format. When you enter a valid 12-hour time without an A or a P, such as 8:30, DOS will default to a.m. Entries for hours, minutes, and seconds are separated with a colon (:) or a period (.).

Examples of usage:

> A:\> TIME 8:30
> (changes the system time to 8:30 a.m.)

> A:\> Time 14:15:35
> (changes the time to 2:15 p.m. and 35 seconds)

> A:\> time 2:15:35p
> (also changes the time to 2:15 p.m. and 35 seconds)

> A:\> TIME 2P
> (changes the time to 2 p.m.)

> A:\> time
> (displays the current time and prompts you to enter a new time)

> A:\> time 11.55.30
> (changes the time to 11:55 a.m. and 30 seconds)

TYPE Command

Syntax: TYPE [d:]filename[.ext]

The **TYPE** command displays the contents of a human-readable file on the standard output device, normally the monitor. It does not alter files. This command is only meaningful when used with ASCII text files, not files that end with an EXE or COM extension. Wildcard characters are not allowed. You can redirect the output to a file or to a printer, as shown in the last example below. Redirection of output is covered in Chapter 9.

Examples of usage:

> A:\> TYPE B:READ.ME
> (displays the contents of B:READ.ME on the monitor)

> A:\> type read.me
> (displays the contents of A:READ.ME on the monitor)

> A:\> TYPE AUTOEXEC.BAT >PRN
> (types the contents of AUTOEXEC.BAT on the printer)

**Using the DOS Shell
to Type (or View) Files**

To send the contents of a text file to the printer, you would have to exit to the system prompt. However, it is relatively easy to display the contents of files on the screen. To view a file, it must first be selected from the File List. Then you can choose the View command from the File pull-down menu to display the contents. If the file is an executable file, only the right part of the screen may be readable. Use what you have learned to view the contents of a text file that you previously created and renamed NEWNAME.TXT.

**VER (Version)
Command**

Syntax: `VER`

The **VER** command displays the DOS version number on the screen, such as MS-DOS Version 6.2. This command is useful if you don't know what version of DOS was used to boot the system.

**VOL (Display Volume
Label) Command**

Syntax: `VOL [d:]`

The **VOL** command displays the internal disk volume label and serial number of the designated drive, if they exist. Use this command to identify a disk once it is inserted into a disk drive. If you do not specify a drive, the default drive is used. Volume labels are created with the FORMAT command and changed with the LABEL command. The LABEL command is covered in the next chapter.

Examples of usage:

`A:\> vol b:`
(displays the volume label recorded on the disk in Drive B; if no label, it displays `Volume in drive B has no label`)

`A:\> VOL`
(displays the volume label of the default disk, Drive A)

Chapter 5

**REVIEW
QUESTIONS**

1. What is the function of brackets in this text for describing the syntax of DOS commands?

2. What is the function of the slash in this text for describing the syntax of DOS commands?

3. What is a delimiter and why is it required?

4. What does the message "Bad command or filename" mean?

5. Where are internal commands stored temporarily?

6. What DOS command erases information from the display screen?

7. What is the benefit of using wildcard characters in the COPY command?

8. What command lets you use the keyboard and printer as a typewriter?

9. What command "deletes" the filename from the disk directory, but does not physically remove the file from the disk?

10. What command displays a directory listing on the screen with filenames in multiple columns?

11. What method is used to get a directory listing of a specific group of files?

12. What command will display all the hidden files on Drive A?

13. What command displays a directory listing of the default disk in sequence by file size (smallest to largest), pausing between screens?

14. What command displays a directory listing of Drive B in descending filename sequence for all files that are *not* read-only?

15. What happens if you include a disk drive designator on both parameters of the RENAME command?

16. What command changes the system time to 4 p.m.?

17. What type of file is considered "listable" with TYPE?

18. What command verifies the DOS version being used?

19. What command displays the internal label on a disk without getting a directory listing?

20. What command erases all the .BAK files on Drive B, prompting you to confirm the deletion of each file?

Chapter 5

FLOPPY DISK LAB EXERCISES

Most of the following exercises can be executed from within the DOS shell. However, Exercises 4 and 5 require that you temporarily exit to the system prompt to enter the commands. Your instructor can decide which approach (the DOS shell or the command line) should be used to complete all the exercises.

1. Boot DOS (Drive A) and insert your data disk in Drive B. Enter **DIR B:** to see the files on Drive B. You should see the COMMAND.COM file, created in Chapter 3 when you formatted your data disk.

2. In this exercise, you will use the COPY CON command to create a small text file.

   • Enter **COPY CON B:READ.ME** (or **copy con b:read.me**).

   • On the lines that follow, enter the following text, pressing the Enter key at the end of each line.

When entering DOS commands, the commands and parameters <Enter>
must be separated by delimiters. Delimiters are normally <Enter>
either a space or a comma. They can be used interchangeably <Enter>
within any command (i.e., COPY A:OLDFILE,B:). <F6><Enter>

- If you have already ended a line that was in error by pressing the Enter key, you cannot correct the error at this time. You can start over completely by pressing Ctrl-C to cancel the COPY command and return to the system prompt.

- After keying the line of text, press function key **F6** (to tell DOS you are finished with the copy operation) and press the Enter key. The text you just keyed is stored on Drive B with the filename of READ.ME. Figure 5.4 shows the screen after you have completed the COPY CON command. The Ctrl-Z (^Z) was created when you pressed the F6 key to identify the end of the file.

Figure 5.4
**Screen Display
of COPY CON**

```
A:\>COPY CON B:READ.ME
When entering DOS commands, the commands and parameters
must be separated by delimiters.  Delimiters are normally
either spaces or commas.  They can used interchangeably
within any command (i.e., COPY A:OLDFILE,B:).^Z
        1 file(s) copied

A:\>
```

3. Enter **COPY B:READ.ME B:TEST.1** and then **COPY B:READ.ME B:TEST.2** to add two more files on Drive B. Then get a directory listing of Drive B in ascending sequence by file size (**DIR B:/OS**). Your screen should now look similar to Figure 5.5.

Figure 5.5
Screen Display
of Sorted Directory

```
C:\DOS>copy b:read.me b:test.1
        1 file(s) copied

C:\DOS>copy b:read.me b:test.2
        1 file(s) copied

C:\DOS>dir b:/os

 Volume in drive B is DOS62
 Volume Serial Number is 141B-13E4
 Directory of B:\

READ     ME          223 01-17-94  12:35p
TEST     1           223 01-17-94  12:35p
TEST     2           223 01-17-94  12:35p
COMMAND  COM      54,619 09-30-93   6:20a
        4 file(s)        55,288 bytes
                        527,360 bytes free

C:\DOS>
```

4. Enter **REN B:TEST.2 TEST.3** to change the filename of TEST.2 on your data disk to TEST.3. Enter **DIR B:** to verify the name change. To simplify the commands in this step, you could have changed the default disk to Drive B before entering the commands.

5. Enter **VOL B:** to see if your data disk has an internal volume label and serial number. If you did not enter a volume label when you formatted the disk, your data disk should not contain one.

6. Enter **VER** to see what version of DOS was used to boot your system. Then enter **DATE** and follow the system prompts to change the current system date. Do the same for **TIME**. You only need to enter hh:mm (e.g., 13:45 or 1:45p) for the time, ignoring seconds.

7. Bonus exercise (requires application of prior learning):

   • Use the COPY command to copy B:TEST.1 to B:TEST.4, using a wildcard character for the target filename. Use DIR to confirm you have five files on Drive B.

   • Using the REN command, change all files on Drive B with a filename of TEST (any extension) to NEWNAME. Use wildcard characters whenever possible. Use the DIR command to confirm the results.

- Now copy all files on Drive B with a filename of NEWNAME to a filename of TEST, without changing the filename extension. Display a directory of the eight files on Drive B to confirm this operation. Finally, delete all files on Drive B with a filename of NEWNAME using the /P option. Your data disk now contains five files: COMMAND.COM, READ.ME, TEST.1, TEST.3, and TEST.4.

This completes the Chapter 5 floppy disk lab exercises. Remove your floppy disk(s) before you leave the computer.

Chapter 5

HARD DISK LAB EXERCISES

Most of the following exercises can be executed from within the DOS shell. However, Exercises 4 and 5 require that you temporarily exit to the system prompt to enter the commands. Your instructor can decide which approach (the DOS shell or the command line) should be used to complete all the exercises.

1. Boot DOS (Drive C) and insert your data disk in Drive A. Enter **DIR** to make sure you are at the subdirectory containing the DOS commands. If you do not see the DOS commands displayed, enter **CD\DOS**. Then enter **DIR A:** to see the files on Drive A. You should see the COMMAND.COM file, created when you formatted your data disk in Chapter 3.

2. In this exercise, you will use the COPY CON command to create a small text file.

   - Enter **COPY CON A:READ.ME** (or **copy con a:read.me**).

   - On the lines that follow, enter the text shown in floppy disk Exercise 2, pressing the Enter key at the end of each line.

   - If you have already ended a line that was in error by pressing the Enter key, you cannot correct the error at this time. You can start over completely by pressing Ctrl-C to cancel the COPY command and return to the system prompt.

   - After keying the last line of text, press function key **F6** (to tell DOS you are finished with the copy operation) and press the Enter key. The text you just keyed is stored on Drive A with the filename of READ.ME. Figure 5.4 above shows the screen after you have completed the COPY CON command. The Ctrl-Z (^Z) was created when you pressed the F6 key to identify the end of the file.

3. Enter **COPY A:READ.ME A:TEST.1** and then **COPY A:READ.ME A:TEST.2** to add two more files on Drive A. Then get a directory listing of Drive A in ascending sequence by file size (**DIR A:/OS**). Your screen should now look similar to Figure 5.5.

4. Enter **REN A:TEST.2 TEST.3** to change the filename of TEST.2 on your data disk to TEST.3. Enter **DIR A:** to verify the name change. To simplify the commands in this step, you could have changed the default disk to Drive A before entering the commands.

5. Enter **VOL A:** to see if your data disk has an internal volume label and serial number. If you did not enter a volume label when you formatted the disk, your data disk should not contain one.

6. Enter **VER** to see what version of DOS was used to boot your system. Then enter **DATE** and follow the system prompts to change the current system date. Do the same for **TIME**. You only need to enter hh:mm (e.g., 13:45 or 1:45p) for the time, ignoring seconds.

7. Bonus exercise (requires application of prior learning):

   - Use the COPY command to copy A:TEST.1 to A:TEST.4, using a wild-card character for the target filename. Use DIR to verify you have five files on Drive A.

   - Using the REN command, change all files on Drive A with a filename of TEST (any extension) to NEWNAME. Use wildcard characters whenever possible. Use the DIR command to confirm the results.

   - Now copy all files on Drive A with a filename of NEWNAME to a filename of TEST, without changing the filename extension. Display a directory of the eight files on Drive A to confirm this operation. Finally, delete all files on Drive A with a filename of NEWNAME using the /P option. Your data disk now contains five files: COMMAND.COM, READ.ME, TEST.1, TEST.3, and TEST.4.

This completes the Chapter 5 hard disk lab exercises. Remove your data disk before you leave the computer.

EXTERNAL DISK COMMANDS

ATTRIB (Attribute) Command

CHKDSK (Check Disk) Command

DISKCOPY Command

LABEL (Volume Label) Command

UNDELETE Command

XCOPY Command

Chapter 6

EXTERNAL DISK COMMANDS

Memory is very precious on a computer, so only the smallest and/or most commonly used DOS commands are internal commands. These commands are part of COMMAND.COM, loaded into RAM when DOS is booted (see Chapter 5). The rest of the DOS commands, called **external commands**, remain on a disk and must be loaded each time they execute.

All external commands have an optional disk drive designator, which DOS uses to find them. For example, suppose the default disk is Drive B and DOS is loaded in Drive A. To execute CHKDSK, enter **A:CHKDSK**. If the designator (i.e., A:) is omitted, DOS looks for the external command on the default drive. The external commands covered in this chapter include:

* **ATTRIB**   Sets the file attributes of a disk file.

  CHKDSK   Provides a disk status report and fixes corrupted disks

* **DISKCOPY**   Makes a duplicate copy of a floppy disk.

  LABEL   Creates, changes, or deletes a disk volume label.

* **UNDELETE** Retrieves accidentally deleted disk files.

  XCOPY   Expanded version of the COPY command.

Note: Commands marked with an asterisk (*) include additional information for using the DOS shell.

ATTRIB (Attribute) Command

Syntax: [d:][path]ATTRIB [+A|-A][+H|-H][+R|-R][d:]filename[.ext] [/S]

The **ATTRIB** command sets file attributes, including archive, hidden, and read-only status. If the ATTRIB command is not on the default drive, the drive designator [d:] is required. The [path] is required for all external commands if the command is not in the current directory. If you enter ATTRIB with no parameters to set attributes, DOS displays the attribute status of the files or disk specified. You may use wildcard characters in the filenames. The **/S** option sets file attributes on a group of directories, and is used with hard disk systems containing subdirectories.

The read-only attribute protects files in a shared or networked environment where you don't want others accidentally destroying your files. If you have important files that you don't want changed, mark them as read-only with ATTRIB. Enter **+R** to set the read-only status on and **−R** to remove it. Files identified as read-only cannot be altered without resetting their status with the ATTRIB command.

Use **+A** or **−A** to set the archive attribute. Commands like BACKUP and XCOPY can selectively copy files that have the archive attribute on (+A).

If you wish to keep certain files from displaying on the normal directory listings, use **+H** to keep them hidden. The +H parameter can also hide a directory name. To remove a hidden status, use the **–H** parameter.

Examples of usage:

    `A:\> ATTRIB +r b:filea.txt`
(sets FILEA.TXT on Drive B to read-only status)

    `A:\> attrib -r B:*.txt`
(sets all files on Drive B with a TXT extension so they are *not* read-only files)

    `A:\> B:attrib +h read.me`
(hides READ.ME on the default drive, using a DOS disk in Drive B)

    `A:\> ATTRIB B:READ.ME`
(displays the file attributes of READ.ME on Drive B)

    `A:\> ATTRIB B:*.*`
(displays the attributes of all files on Drive B)

    `A:\> ATTRIB +R A:COMMAND.COM`
(helps to protect your COMMAND.COM file from being adversely affected by some computer viruses by setting it to read-only)

    `A:\> attrib +a b:memo.*`
(turns on the archive attribute for all files on Drive B named MEMO)

    `C:\> ATTRIB +H \GAMES`
(hides the GAMES directory on Drive C)

Using the DOS Shell to View and/or Change File Attributes

To *view attributes* of a file that has been selected and highlighted in the File List, choose the **Show Information** option from the **Options** pull-down menu. You can exit from the dialog box by pressing the Esc key.

To *change attributes* of the selected file, choose the **Change Attributes** option from the **File** pull-down menu. Exit from the dialog box, executing the changes, by choosing the OK command button. If you exit with the Esc key, no changes are made.

Using what you have learned, use the DOS shell to do the following practice exercises:

1. Move to the File List area and select the Format command.

2. Using the Show Information option, view its attributes.

3. Using the Change Attributes option, change the Format command to be a read-only file. Then view its attributes again.

**Selecting More
Than One File
from a File List**

You may sometimes wish to execute a command on a group of files without using wildcard characters. The DOS shell lets you do this within the set of files displayed in the File List as follows:

1. To select all the files in the File List, choose the Select All option in the File pull-down menu.

2. To select a subset of two or more files that are listed together (in sequence), use the Shift key. Highlight the first file in the sequence and hold down the Shift key as you highlight the rest of the files you want selected, one at a time. This approach works with a mouse, or with the Up and Down arrow keys.

3. The process of selecting two or more files that are not in sequence is a bit more complicated using the keyboard.

   KEYBOARD: Press the Shift-F8 key combination after selecting the first file in the File List. The message "Add" displays in the status bar. Use the arrow keys to locate the next file and select it by pressing the space bar. After all files have been selected, press Shift-F8 to exit from the "add mode."

   MOUSE: Press and hold down the Ctrl key (continuously) while you click the name of each file you want to select, including the first file.

After performing the desired actions for a group of files, you may wish to "deselect" them before doing your next operation. To do this, choose the **Deselect** option from the **File** pull-down menu.

**CHKDSK (Check Disk)
Command**

Syntax: `[d:][path]CHKDSK [d:][filename[.ext]] [/F] [/V]`

The **CHKDSK** command produces a disk status report for a specified disk and lists the memory status of the system. The **/F** option fixes problems in the File Allocation Table. The **/V** option displays the full filenames of all files on a specified drive. After checking the disk, CHKDSK displays a status report and any error messages. Figure 6.1 is an example of a CHKDSK report for a 720KB floppy disk.

Figure 6.1

Sample CHKDSK Report

```
C:\DOS>chkdsk b:

Volume SOUTHWORTH  created 01-17-1994 12:42p
Volume Serial Number is 141B-13E4

    730,112 bytes total disk space
    144,384 bytes in 3 hidden files
     59,392 bytes in 5 user files
    526,336 bytes available on disk

      1,024 bytes in each allocation unit
        713 total allocation units on disk
        514 available allocation units on disk

    655,360 total bytes memory
    560,656 bytes free

Instead of using CHKDSK, try using SCANDISK.  SCANDISK can reliably detect
and fix a much wider range of disk problems.  For more information,
type HELP SCANDISK from the command prompt.

C:\DOS>
```

The three hidden files in the status report represent DOS system files that are hidden from normal directory lists. The bottom portion of the report represents the memory status. It shows total memory and the number of free bytes. The bytes used represents the amount of RAM allocated to the resident portion of DOS 6, plus the space required to load CHKDSK.

A file is written to contiguous allocation units if the first unallocated space is big enough to hold it. Otherwise, DOS uses whatever areas it finds to store a file, skipping over allocated areas. Consequently, files can easily become fragmented.

If you specify a filename or group of files, CHKDSK displays the number of noncontiguous areas occupied by the file(s). Wildcard characters are allowed in the filename. For example, you can use *.* to see the extent of file fragmentation on a given directory of a disk. To improve access speed when files are fragmented, run the DEFRAG command (see Chapter 8).

Lost allocation clusters are parts of files, allocated in the File Allocation Table (FAT), yet absent in the disk's directory. Specifically, the first cluster number in a chain is missing. This discrepancy occurs because of some malfunction during the file saving process. It can be caused by a loss of power or by resetting the computer during a disk write operation.

You can use the /F option to combine lost clusters on a disk into a file named FILEnnnn.CHK, where nnnn is a unique number. This is a good command to use periodically. When the FAT is corrupted, it cannot accurately track files on disk. Whenever CHKDSK /F finds any lost clusters, you will see an error message similar to this:

```
6 lost clusters found in 2 chains.

Convert lost chains to files (Y/N)?
```

In this example, CHKDSK determined that lost data came from two different files (or two parts of the same file). If you respond **Y**, a CHK file is created for each chain. If a CHK file created by CHKDSK is listable, you can use TYPE to view the lost data. After identifying the lost data, you should delete all CHK files to make room for other files on the disk. If you respond **N**, DOS removes the lost clusters, but it doesn't save the contents for you to see. Because Windows 3.1 uses a lot of temporary files, you cannot execute CHKDSK /F while Windows is running.

When you use CHKDSK *without the /F option* and errors are detected, you must run it again with the /F option to fix those errors. Disk errors should be fixed before you continue to use the disk. The problems can only get worse if you wait. Use CHKDSK whenever the following conditions occur:

- Unexpected data appears within a file or on a directory listing.

- A program fails to run as it should.

- You suspect disk damage after major problems, such as a power failure or a system lockup.

Beginning with Version 6.2 of DOS, an improved disk repair command was added to replace the limited "fix" capabilities of CHKDSK. This command, called SCANDISK, is covered in Chapter 8. If SCANDISK is available, use it to fix any errors reported by CHKDSK.

Examples of usage:

    A:\> CHKDSK
(displays a status report for the default drive)

    A:\> chkdsk /f
(displays a status report for Drive A and fixes any errors found in the FAT)

    A:\> b:chkdsk a:*.*
(loads CHKDSK from Drive B, displays a status report for Drive A, and lists any fragmented files found on Drive A)

    A:\> chkdsk B:
(displays a status report for Drive B and displays the number of noncontiguous areas contained in READ.ME)

    C:\WORD\FILES> CHKDSK *.*
(displays a status report identifying any fragmented files in the FILES subdirectory)

DISKCOPY Command   Syntax: [d:][path]DISKCOPY d: d: [/V]

Unlike the COPY command, which duplicates files, DISKCOPY duplicates floppy disks. The **DISKCOPY** command copies the contents of an entire floppy disk, track by track and sector by sector, to another disk of the same density.

If the source disk has a volume serial number, DOS creates a different one for the target disk. If you specify only one drive as the source and target disk, Version 6.2 of DOS uses the hard disk (if available) as a work space. Thus, it can duplicate a floppy disk without your having to switch disks. Unlike the COPY command, DISKCOPY duplicates system and hidden files. It also duplicates fragmented files, without removing the fragmentation. Because DISKCOPY destroys all files on the target disk, you should use this command only when you do not wish to save any of the files on the target disk.

DISKCOPY is one of the few commands (other than FORMAT) that can format a disk if required. When duplicating a disk to an unformatted one, any bad sectors on the target disk (those normally bypassed by using COPY) are written to during DISKCOPY, resulting in lost data. In addition, any bad sectors noted on the source disk are marked as bad on the target disk. Error messages display if errors are detected. Use the /V option to verify that a disk created with DISKCOPY is identical to the source disk.

Examples of usage:

A:\> DISKCOPY A: B:
(makes a copy of the disk in Drive A onto a disk in Drive B; the target disk does not need to be formatted)

A:\> diskcopy a:/v
(makes an exact copy of the source disk inserted in Drive A onto a target disk to be inserted into Drive A, verifying that the copy was accurate)

Using the DOS Shell to Copy Disks

To copy one floppy disk to another of the same type, you first need to access the Disk Utilities entry in the Main program menu area. Then choose Disk Copy and follow the directions to copy the disks.

LABEL (Volume Label) Command

Syntax: [d:][path]LABEL [d:] [volume label]

The **LABEL** command lets you create, change, or delete a volume label on a disk. It is a good idea to label your disks internally. Then you can identify them using the VOL command without having to remove the disk from a drive to read an external label attached to the disk. DOS also displays the volume label when you run the DIR, CHKDSK, or TREE commands. If you do not specify a volume label, DOS displays the current label. It then prompts you to enter a label or press the Enter key to delete the current label.

Examples of usage:

A:\> Label b:fred
(creates a volume label of FRED on the disk in Drive B)

B:\> A:LABEL FRED
(also creates a volume label of FRED on the disk in Drive B)

A:\> LABEL
(displays the current volume label on the default drive and prompts you to modify it)

UNDELETE Command Syntax: [d:][path]UNDELETE [[d:]filename[.ext]] [/LIST]

The **UNDELETE** command restores files deleted with the DEL command. You can selectively undelete files by specifying the filename. Wildcard characters are permitted. If no filenames are specified, UNDELETE lets you restore all deleted files, prompting you for confirmation on each file. The **/LIST** option lists deleted files, but it does not undelete any files.

UNDELETE only restores deleted files if the space freed in the FAT has not yet been used by other files. *Whenever you accidentally delete a file, use the UNDELETE command immediately, before the data gets overwritten.* Figure 6.2 shows a screen display of an UNDELETE operation. More information on UNDELETE is provided in Chapter 8.

Figure 6.2
Screen Display of an
UNDELETE Process

```
UNDELETE - A delete protection facility
Copyright (C) 1987-1993 Central Point Software, Inc.
All rights reserved.

Directory: A:\
File Specifications: *.*

    Delete Sentry control file not found.

    Deletion-tracking file not found.

    MS-DOS directory contains    1 deleted files.
    Of those,    1 files may be recovered.
Using the MS-DOS directory method.

        ?ESTFILE TXT      140  7-24-93 11:01a  ...A  Undelete (Y/N)?Y
        Please type the first character for ?ESTFILE.TXT: T

File successfully undeleted.

A:\>
```

Examples of usage:

```
A:\> undelete b:/list
```
(lists any deleted files on Drive B)

```
A:\> UNDELETE B:*.DOC
```
(lets you restore any deleted DOC files on Drive B)

```
A:\> UNDELETE B:
```
(lets you undelete all files marked as deleted on Drive B)

Using the DOS Shell to Undelete Files

The Undelete option is included in the Disk Utilities submenu in the Main program menu area. It can identify the deleted files in the currently selected directory (the one highlighted in the Directory Tree). The default command parameter in the text box is the /LIST option.

To undelete a file in the current directory, enter the appropriate parameter into the text box, such as *.* or *.BAK. If the undelete process was successful, you should tell DOS to reread the disk's directory to include the undelete file(s) on the File List. Do so by choosing the Refresh option on the View pull-down menu.

Possibly there is a deleted file on your current DOS directory. Use the Undelete option (with /LIST as the parameter) to find out which files on the DOS directory have a deleted status. After identifying the deleted file(s), use the Undelete option to recover one of them. Then, refresh the screen to cause the recovered file(s) to show in the File List.

XCOPY Command

Syntax: [d:][path]XCOPY [d:]filename[.ext] [[d:][filename[.ext]][/M] [/P] [/S]

The **XCOPY** command is used to selectively copy files and directories, including any lower-level subdirectories and their files. The first filename in the syntax represents the source filename(s), and the second filename identifies the target filename(s). Whenever you do not specify a disk drive or path, DOS uses normal default values. If you do not specify a target file, DOS copies to the default directory using the same filenames as the source files. If the specified path does not exist on the target disk, XCOPY creates the directories as it copies files to those directories.

The source can include multiple files with the use of wildcard characters. Like the COPY command, it will not copy hidden files or replace matching read-only files. Unlike COPY, XCOPY can't copy to or from devices like PRN and CON. Beginning with Version 6.2, XCOPY warns you before it writes over a file with data from a file with the same name.

XCOPY uses an effective buffering technique to copy files. Multiple files are read into RAM (as much as RAM will hold) and then copied to the target disk as a group. When you have many files to copy, this approach is faster than using COPY, which copies only one file at a time. The execution options provided give XCOPY power and flexibility.

The **/M** option copies only files that have their archive attribute set on. These files have not yet been backed up. Once the files are copied, the archive attribute is turned off. This option makes it easy to copy many files onto multiple backup disks. You can set the archive attribute on files by using the ATTRIB command with the +A parameter. When using XCOPY /M, as each backup disk fills, the archive attribute is set off for each file copied. This command is repeated until there are no more source files with the archive attribute on.

The **/P** option prompts you with a message allowing you to selectively confirm whether you want to copy each file. This option lets you issue a single XCOPY command with wildcard characters and then selectively copy desired files from that set of files.

The **/S** option copies files from directories, including all lower-level subdirectories. *If you omit this option, DOS only copies files in the single directory specified.* If a target directory does not exist, DOS automatically creates one.

Examples of usage:

A:\> XCOPY \word*.DOC b:\bkup\
(copies all files in the WORD directory on the default disk to a directory on Drive B named \BKUP, without changing any filenames)

C:\DOS> xcopy *.* b:/m/s
(copies all files in all directories and subdirectories of Drive C with their archive attribute on to Drive B)

C:\DOS> XCOPY A:*.* B:*.BAK /S/P
(copies all files on Drive A, from all directories, to Drive B, changing the extensions to BAK and pausing to confirm that each file should be copied)

C:\DOS> xcopy command.com \
(copies the COMMAND.COM file from the DOS directory to the root directory)

C:\LOTUS> XCOPY *.WK? A:/S
(copies all the spreadsheet files on the default directory, and its lower directories, to Drive A)

Chapter 6

REVIEW QUESTIONS

1. What distinguishes external commands from internal commands?

2. What command sets B:MEMO.DOC to read-only status?

3. What command shows you the file attributes for all files on Drive A?

4. What are the hidden files you would expect to find on a system disk?

5. What command protects the COMMAND.COM file from being changed?

6. What command turns off the archive attribute for all BAK files on Drive B?

7. Describe the process to select more than one file in a File List when using the DOS shell with a mouse.

8. How can you determine the amount of file fragmentation on a disk?

9. What two commands can be used to fix a corrupted FAT?

10. Define a "lost allocation cluster" on a disk.

11. What are the primary differences between using the COPY command and using the DISKCOPY command?

12. How can the internal volume label be changed without reformatting the disk?

13. When should the /F option not be used with the CHKDSK command?

14. What is contained in a file called FILE0001.CHK?

15. What command lists all the deleted files on Drive B?

16. Under what circumstances would you be unable to successfully undelete a previously deleted file?

17. What command restores B:MEMO.DOC if you accidentally delete it?

18. In what ways are the COPY command and the XCOPY command the same?

19. In what ways are COPY and XCOPY different?

20. What benefits could there be of placing all of an application's data files in separate subdirectories?

Chapter 6

FLOPPY DISK LAB EXERCISES

Most of the following exercises can be executed within the DOS shell. Your instructor can decide which approach (the shell or command line) should be used to complete these exercises.

1. Boot DOS (Drive A) and insert your data disk into Drive B. Enter **DIR B:** to verify the contents of Drive B. Enter **ATTRIB +R B:TEST.3** to set a file to a read-only status. Enter **ATTRIB B:*.*** to verify that it was changed correctly. If done correctly, TEST.1 and TEST.4 will not indicate a read-only status and TEST.3 will be a read-only file. An R is displayed to the left of read-only filenames (S indicates a system file). Figure 6.3 shows what the screen should look like at this point in the exercise.

Figure 6.3
Screen Display of DIR and
ATTRIB [new]

```
    Volume in drive B is SOUTHWORTH
    Volume Serial Number is 141B-13E4
    Directory of B:\

COMMAND  COM        54,619 09-30-93   6:20a
READ     ME            223 01-17-94  12:35p
TEST     1             223 01-17-94  12:35p
TEST     3             223 01-17-94  12:35p
TEST     4             223 01-17-94  12:35p
         5 file(s)          55,511 bytes
                           526,336 bytes free


C:\DOS>attrib +r b:test.3

C:\DOS>attrib b:*.*
   A   SHR    B:\IO.SYS
   A   SHR    B:\MSDOS.SYS
   A          B:\COMMAND.COM
   A   SHR    B:\DBLSPACE.BIN
   A          B:\READ.ME
   A          B:\TEST.1
   A     R    B:\TEST.3
   A          B:\TEST.4

C:\DOS>
```

2. If you are not certain about the syntax of a DOS command, you can get help by entering the command name followed by the /? option. Use this option with several external commands discussed in this chapter (e.g., ATTRIB /?).

3. To give a disk on Drive B a volume label, enter **LABEL B:** and follow the system prompts to enter a label of up to 11 characters (e.g., DATADISK). Enter **VOL B:** to verify the new volume label. Does your DOS disk have a volume label? Use the VOL command to check, but don't try to change it.

4. Enter **ATTRIB +H B:TEST.*** to hide all the files on Drive B that have a file-name of TEST. Enter **DIR B:** to display a directory listing of Drive B without including these hidden files. Now enter the same command with the **/AH** option to display only the hidden files. Enter **ATTRIB -H B:TEST.*** to reset the hidden attribute so these files will normally be included in directory listings.

5. Enter **CHKDSK** to get a status report of the default drive (A:). Then enter **CHKDSK B:*.*** to get a status report of your data disk, directing the system to check for any fragmented files. Figure 6.4 shows the display screen after running CHKDSK. Your display screen should look similar to this one.

Figure 6.4
Screen Display of CHKDSK

```
C:\DOS>chkdsk b:*.*

Volume SOUTHWORTH  created 01-17-1994 12:42p
Volume Serial Number is 141B-13E4

     730,112 bytes total disk space
     144,384 bytes in 3 hidden files
      59,392 bytes in 5 user files
     526,336 bytes available on disk

       1,024 bytes in each allocation unit
         713 total allocation units on disk
         514 available allocation units on disk

     655,360 total bytes memory
     560,656 bytes free

All specified file(s) are contiguous

Instead of using CHKDSK, try using SCANDISK.  SCANDISK can reliably detect
and fix a much wider range of disk problems.  For more information,
type HELP SCANDISK from the command prompt.


C:\DOS>
```

6. Delete all the TEST files on Drive B. Enter **UNDELETE B:/LIST** to see what files were deleted on Drive B. Your screen should look something like Figure 6.5. Then, enter **UNDELETE B:TEST.*** to restore them. Follow the instructions to undelete files and restore the first character of the filename (T). Finally, get a directory listing of Drive B to verify that the files were restored correctly.

Figure 6.5
Screen Display
of UNDELETE

```
C:\DOS>del b:test.*

C:\DOS>undelete b:/list

UNDELETE - A delete protection facility
Copyright (C) 1987-1993 Central Point Software, Inc.
All rights reserved.

Directory: B:\
File Specifications: *.*

    Delete Sentry control file not found.

    Deletion-tracking file not found.

    MS-DOS directory contains    2 deleted files.
    Of those,    2 files may be recovered.

Using the MS-DOS directory method.

        ?EST     1       223  1-17-94 12:35p  ...A
        ?EST     4       223  1-17-94 12:35p  ...A
C:\DOS>
```

7. Bonus exercise (requires application of prior learning):

- Copy B:TEST.1 to B:TEST.ROF. Set the new file to read-only status and try to delete it. Then reset the read-only attribute to allow writing to the file. Set the hidden file attribute of B:TEST.ROF to make it a hidden file and use the DIR command to verify that it is hidden. Before you continue, do whatever is required to delete B:TEST.ROF, and then restore it with the UNDELETE command.

- Use the LABEL command to eliminate the volume label on your data disk. Use the VOL command to confirm that the label is no longer there. Then change it back to its previous value. Use the DIR command to confirm the change. This shows that at least three commands display a disk's volume label. What is another DOS command that displays the label?

This concludes the Chapter 6 floppy disk lab exercises. Remove your floppy disk(s) before you leave the computer.

Chapter 6

HARD DISK LAB EXERCISES

Most of the following exercises can be executed within the DOS shell. Your instructor can decide which approach (the shell or command line) should be used to complete these exercises.

1. Boot DOS (Drive C) and insert your data disk into Drive A. If you are not at the DOS portion of the hard disk, enter **CD\DOS**. Enter **DIR A:** to verify the contents of Drive A. Enter **ATTRIB +R A:TEST.3** to set a file to read-only status. Enter **ATTRIB A:*.*** to verify that it was changed correctly. If done correctly, TEST.1 and TEST.4 will not indicate a read-only status and TEST.3 will be a read-only file. An R is displayed to the left of read-only filenames (S indicates a system file). Figure 6.3 shows what the screen should look similar to at this point in the exercise.

2. If you are not certain about the syntax of a DOS command, you can get help by entering the command name followed by the /? option. Use this option with several external commands discussed in this chapter (e.g., ATTRIB /?).

3. To give a disk on Drive A a volume label, enter **LABEL A:** and follow the system prompts to enter a label of up to 11 characters (e.g., DATADISK). Enter **VOL A:** to verify the new volume label. Does your DOS disk have a volume label? Use the VOL command to check, but don't try to change it.

4. To hide all the files on Drive A that have a filename of TEST, enter **ATTRIB +H A:TEST.***. To display a directory listing of Drive A without including these hidden files, enter **DIR A:**. Now enter the same command with the **/AH** option to display only the hidden files. Enter **ATTRIB -H A:TEST.*** to reset the hidden attribute so these files will normally be included in directory listings.

5. Enter **CHKDSK** to get a status report of the default drive (C:). Then enter **CHKDSK A:*.*** to get a status report of your data disk, directing the system to check for any fragmented files. Figure 6.4 shows the display screen after running CHKDSK. Your display screen should look similar to this one.

6. Delete all the TEST files on Drive A. Enter **UNDELETE A:/LIST** to see what files were deleted on Drive A. Your screen should look something like Figure 6.5. Then, enter **UNDELETE A:TEST.*** to restore them. Follow the instructions to undelete files and restore the first character of the filename (T). Finally, get a directory listing of Drive A to verify that the files were restored correctly.

7. Backing up hard disk files to floppy disks can be time-consuming. But backing up just the essential files is much better than no backup at all. Often this process requires many floppy disks. Use the following set of commands as many times as required, substituting a desired subdirectory name (e.g., C:\DOS) for "xxxxxx" to back up all files on that subdirectory to Drive A:

ATTRIB +A xxxxxx   (sets the archive attribute on for all files)

XCOPY xxxxxx A:/M (copies all files with archive attribute on, turning off each file attribute as it copies)

8. Bonus exercise (requires application of prior learning):

- Copy A:TEST.1 to A:TEST.ROF. Set the new file to read-only status and try to delete it. Then reset the read-only attribute to allow writing to the file. Set the hidden file attribute of A:TEST.ROF to make it a hidden file and use the DIR command to verify that it is hidden. Before you continue, do whatever is required to delete A:TEST.ROF, and then restore it with the UNDELETE command.

- Use the LABEL command to eliminate the volume label on your data disk. Use the VOL command to confirm that the label is no longer there. Then change it back to its previous value. Use the DIR command to confirm the change. This shows that there are at least three commands that display a disk's volume label. What is another DOS command that displays the label?

This concludes the Chapter 6 hard disk lab exercises. Remove your data disk before you leave the computer.

HARD DISK MANAGEMENT

The management of files on hard disks is different from that of floppy disks. Floppy disk files are organized manually by grouping files on a disk and identifying each disk with an external label. Hard disks are organized "electronically" into subdirectories. This facilitates working with many files on hard disks. Directories and subdirectories are logical work areas on a hard disk.

This chapter teaches you how to work with subdirectories using commands primarily related to hard disks. The sample structure (hierarchy) of subdirectories in Figure 7.1 is referenced throughout this chapter. The term *directory* is often used to represent *subdirectory*, as a subdirectory is simply a lower-level directory.

Figure 7.1

**Sample Hierarchy
of Subdirectories**

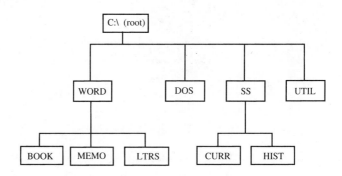

WORKING WITH SUBDIRECTORIES

DOS uses a preceding backslash (\) before a directory name to represent the break between one level in the hierarchy and the next level. Thus, the file BOSS.DOC stored in the MEMO directory is identified with the full filename C:\WORD\MEMO\BOSS.DOC. The following examples show how the backslash identifies directories:

\   The root directory.

\WORD   The WORD directory under the root.

\WORD\MEMO   The MEMO directory under the WORD directory under
                  the root.

The full filename includes the **path** of directories that must be followed by DOS to find the file in the hierarchy. If the path is not included in the filename, DOS looks for the file on the current directory. The **current (or default) directory** is the directory you are currently using. DOS treats the current directory as the default path, similar to the default disk concept. The current directory is used whenever a directory is not specified. Here are some examples with C:\DOS as the current directory:

```
C:\DOS> DIR
```
(displays just the files in the DOS directory)

```
C:\DOS> CHKDSK *.*
```
(checks for file fragmentation in the DOS directory only)

```
C:\DOS> CHKDSK \*.*
```
(checks for file fragmentation in the root directory of Drive C)

A backslash at the beginning of the path tells DOS to begin looking for the directory from the root. If the backslash is not included, DOS starts looking from the current directory. You must provide DOS the path to find files not in the current directory, or you will get a "File not found" message. The path is part of the full filename, as is the disk designator when a file is not on the default drive.

It is advantageous to set up directories so that program files are separate from data files. You can back up the directories containing data files (which change frequently) without having to back up program files (which do not change). Directories containing program files need to be backed up only once, unless programs are added or upgraded.

DOS has several commands that let you create and use directories. You can change to any directory from the system prompt. Directories on hard disks can have many entries, including filenames and subdirectory names. When you use the DIR command, directories are shown with the symbol <DIR>. Because directory names typically do not have extensions, the command **DIR *.** displays all the directories in the current directory. Directory listings have a "dot" and a "double-dot" directory entry, sometimes called directory markers, like this:

```
.       <DIR>    8-15-92    9:45a
..      <DIR>    8-15-92    9:45a
```

The single dot represents the current directory. Although the single dot is not a commonly documented feature, it can be used in place of *.*. For example, the command **COPY . B:** copies all files from the current directory to Drive B. The double dot represents the **parent directory**, one level up from the current directory. It is often used as shorthand notation to reference a parent directory. For example, if you are at the C:\SS\HIST directory, the command **CD..** changes to the SS directory.

The following suggestions may prevent disk management problems when you are setting up your hard disk directory structure:

- Do not store any unnecessary programs or data files in the root directory. Normally, only a few files need to be in the root directory: the hidden system files, COMMAND.COM, AUTOEXEC.BAT, and CONFIG.SYS.

- Do not assign extensions to your *directory* names.

- Do not give your directories long or confusing names. Although directory names can be up to eight characters, give them short and meaningful names, such as: DOS, WP, DB, SS, and so on.

- Do not create directories more than two levels below the root directory.

HARD DISK COMMANDS

The hard disk commands are introduced in the following logical sequence:

*CD	(Change Directory) Changes to another directory.
*MD	(Make Directory) Creates a directory.
RD	(Remove Directory) Deletes a directory.
DELTREE	(Delete Tree) Lets you delete a directory plus all files and directories in that directory.
*MOVE	Used to move files between directories and/or disk drives.
PATH	Instructs DOS where to look for command files.
PROMPT	Changes the system prompt.
TREE	Displays the complete directory tree structure.

Note: Commands marked with an asterisk (*) include additional information for using the DOS shell.

The format for all commands designated as external below includes the optional parameters [d:][path] just before the command. These parameters designate the disk drive and the directory path DOS needs to find the external command.

CD (Change Directory) Command (internal) — also CHDIR

Syntax: CD [d:][path]

The **CD** command lets you change from the current directory to another one. The path identifies the directory you want to change to. For example, if you want to change to the root directory, you enter CD\. A leading backslash (\) in the path directs DOS to start the search path at the root directory. Normally, you want to start at the root directory to help DOS find the directory. Entering the CD command with no parameters displays the current directory.

You can save keystrokes by recognizing that the symbols \ and .. are considered delimiters in DOS commands, just like a space and a slash (/). Thus, the commands CD\ and CD \ are the same.

Examples of usage:

`C:\DOS> CD \`
(changes to the root directory)

`C:\DOS> Cd`
(displays the current directory)

`C:\DOS> cd\word\memo`
(changes to the directory named MEMO on the WORD directory, starting from the root directory)

`C:\> CD WORD\MEMO`
(changes to the directory named MEMO on the WORD directory, starting from the current directory)

`C:\DOS> cd..`
(changes to the parent directory)

Using the DOS Shell to Change Directories

To change to a different directory, select the new directory in the Directory Tree. When you start the shell, only the first-level directories are displayed. A plus (+) sign next to a directory name indicates that the directory contains one or more subdirectories. If a subdirectory you want to change to is not included in the tree listing, you can expand the directory listings as follows:

KEYBOARD: Select the directory you want to expand and press the plus (+) key.

MOUSE: Click on the plus (+) sign next to the name of the appropriate directory.

To view all directory levels on the current disk, choose the **Expand All** option from the **Tree** pull-down menu. When a directory is expanded, a minus sign (–) displays next to the directory name. To collapse a directory, you can use the same process for expanding with one exception: use a minus sign instead of a plus sign.

MD (Make Directory) Command (internal) — also MKDIR

Syntax: `MD [d:]path`

The **MD** command creates a directory in a given location. You may create as many directories as you want, but keep in mind that too many directories can cause confusion. Directory names must be unique within a directory.

Examples of usage:

> C:\DOS> MD\word
>
> (creates a directory named WORD one level down from the root directory, as shown in Figure 7.1)
>
> C:\DOS> md \word\MEMO
>
> (creates a directory named MEMO one level down from the directory named WORD, as shown in Figure 7.1)
>
> C:\> Md games
>
> (creates a directory called GAMES one level down from the current directory, which is the root directory in this example)

Using the DOS Shell to Create Directories

To simplify the process of creating a subdirectory, begin by selecting the parent directory as the current directory. Then choose the **Create Directory** option from the **File** pull-down menu. After entering the subdirectory name in the text box, press the Enter key (or click on the OK command button) to create the new directory.

RD (Remove Directory) Command (internal) — also RMDIR

Syntax: RD [d:]path

The **RD** command removes a directory from a disk. Before you can remove a directory it must be empty (no files or subdirectories). DOS will remove the directory markers (the . and .. directories) automatically. You must change to another directory before removing the current directory. Therefore, you can never remove the root directory. Refer to the DELTREE command, covered next, for another method of removing directories.

Examples of usage:

> C:\DOS> rd \word\memo
>
> (removes the directory named MEMO from the WORD directory)
>
> C:\WORD> rd memo
>
> (removes the directory named MEMO from the current directory, WORD)
>
> C:\> RD \WORD
>
> (removes the WORD directory from the root directory)

Using the DOS Shell to Remove Directories

The DOS shell has a handy feature not available from the command line. If you wish to remove a directory that is empty, select the directory (using the keyboard or mouse) and press the Del key. If it is empty, DOS will ask you to confirm that you wish to delete the selected directory. Press Y (or select Yes) to remove the directory.

DELTREE (Delete Tree) Command (external)

Syntax: DELTREE [d:]path

The **DELTREE** command removes a specified directory (path), all of its subdirectories, and all of the files in the directories. Before DOS 6, you had to delete all files in a directory, and then use the RD command to remove the empty directory. DELTREE lets you remove directories that are full. Like the MD command, you must change to another directory before removing the current one.

This powerful and potentially destructive command should be used very carefully. As a small measure of protection, DELTREE prompts you with the message "Delete directory <dirname> and all of its subdirectories?" In addition, you are prompted for each file on the directory you are deleting, but not its subdirectories. The major potential problems are:

- You can use wildcard characters with DELTREE, but use them with caution. Any directories (and their files) that match the wildcards are deleted.

- Files in a deleted directory cannot be undeleted.

- DELTREE deletes files regardless of the attribute settings.

Therefore, we recommend that you use the DIR command with the /S option to view all of the files on any subdirectories you plan on deleting before using DELTREE.

Examples of usage:

C:\DOS> deltree \bkup
(deletes the directory C:\BKUP, including all of its files and subdirectories)

C:\DOS> DELTREE A:*.*
(deletes all files and subdirectories on Drive A)

C:\DOS> DELTREE \WORD\MEMO
(deletes all subdirectories and files associated with MEMO, including the MEMO directory, leaving \WORD unchanged)

C:\WORD\MEMO> DELTREE \WORD\MEMO
(deletes all subdirectories and files associated with MEMO, leaving the current directory, MEMO, a subdirectory of \WORD)

MOVE Command (external)

Syntax: `MOVE [d:][path]filename[.ext] [d:][path]filename[.ext]`

The MOVE command is a powerful file management command, but with some limitations. The **MOVE** command moves a file to the location you specify. It functions similar to other commands you know in combination. For example, we can "move" FILEA by using the COPY command to create FILEB, and then use the DEL command to delete FILEA. The MOVE command is more efficient for this type of operation. When a file is moved on the same disk, it does not need to be physically copied. Only the full filename is changed on the disk's directory, reflecting the new name. **Note:** the REN command only changes the name of a file on a directory; it cannot rename it to another directory like the MOVE command.

The MOVE command can also rename directories, when both the source and target directories belong to the same parent directory. Because MOVE does not restructure the directory hierarchy of a disk, you cannot move a directory to another branch in the tree.

Wildcard characters can be used to move a group of files at a time. However, it only allows you to move multiple files if they keep their original names. Thus, you cannot move *and* rename multiple files with a single command.

Examples of usage:

`C:\DOS> MOVE \WORD\MEMO\BOSS.DOC \WORD\LTR`
(moves BOSS.DOC on the \WORD\MEMO directory to the \WORD\LTR directory without changing the filename)

`C:\DOS> MOVE \WORD\MEMO\BOSS.DOC \WORD\LTR\BOSS.BAK`
(moves BOSS.DOC on the \WORD\MEMO directory to the \WORD\LTR directory, changing the filename to BOSS.BAK)

`C:\DOS> move \word\memo\*.doc \word\ltr`
(moves all DOC files on C:\WORD\MEMO to C:\WORD\LTR without changing any filenames)

`C:\DOS> move format.com formatx.com`
(renames FORMAT.COM to FORMATX.COM on the current directory)

`C:\DOS> MOVE \WORD\LTR \WORD\LETTER`
(renames the \WORD\LTR directory on Drive C to \WORD\LETTER)

Using the DOS Shell to Move (Rename) Files

Once a file or a directory in the shell window is highlighted, it can be "moved" by renaming it. Choose the Rename command from the File pull-down menu to move the selected file or directory. In addition, by using a mouse you can "drag and drop" a file from the File List area to another disk drive or a directory.

To drag and drop a file, you must first position the mouse pointer on the file-name to be moved in the File List. While holding down the left mouse button, drag the mouse pointer to a different disk icon or a different directory name in the Directory area. When you drag a file, the mouse pointer changes temporarily from the arrow symbol. When you release the left mouse button, you are prompted to confirm the move operation. Responding "Y" to the prompt will result in the file being dropped at the new location.

PATH (Set Search Path) Command (internal)

Syntax: `PATH [d:][path][;path][;path]`

When you enter a command that is not an internal command, DOS searches the current directory (or the one specified in the command) for it. The **PATH** command directs DOS to search one or more directories for commands not found in the current directory. With a tree-structured directory, you cannot always access a command just by entering the command name. If it resides on a directory other than the current directory, you must specify the path so DOS can find it. The PATH command tells DOS what directories to search, and in what order, to find a command not on the current directory.

PATH should be added to your AUTOEXEC.BAT file so that it automatically executes every time you boot DOS. In addition, it is a good idea to store DOS commands in a directory named \DOS. This is because DOS automatically sets the search path to C:\DOS if (1) you fail to set the path in your AUTOEXEC.BAT file, and (2) if a directory named \DOS exists on drive C.

PATH locates only executable files, those with an extension of COM, EXE, or BAT. In each directory, DOS always looks for a matching command with a COM extension first. If it does not find one, DOS searches for an EXE extension, and finally a BAT extension. Whenever DOS cannot find the command to execute, it displays the message, "Bad command or filename."

The following important points relate to the PATH command:

● The search path is created with the PATH command.

● You may only have one search path active at a time.

● Directories are searched in the order they are listed in the search path.

● Typing mistakes in the path are not flagged as errors.

● Typing the command PATH with no parameters displays the current path.

● The command PATH; tells the system you do not want any search path.

● Issuing a PATH command does not change the current directory.

● The search path is limited to 127 characters in length.

Examples of usage:

C:\DOS> Path C:\DOS
(directs the system to look in the directory named DOS, if it cannot find a command in the current directory)

C:\DOS> PATH C:\WORD\LTRS
(directs DOS to look in LTRS within WORD to find a command, if it is not in the current directory)

C:\DOS> path
(displays the current search path setting)

C:\DOS> Path ;
(deletes the current search path setting)

C:\DOS> PATH C:\DOS;C:\UTIL;C:\
(directs DOS to search three directories in the order given: \DOS, \UTIL, and then the root directory)

PROMPT (Set System Prompt) Command (internal)

Syntax: PROMPT [text]

where text is a variable-length string of characters. Text often contains special codes that begin with a dollar sign. Here are seven of the most commonly used codes:

$t The system time

$d The system date

$n The default (current) drive

$g The > character

$_ The "new line" command (to skip a line)

$p The default disk and current directory

$e Sends an escape code (see Chapter 11)

The **PROMPT** command changes the appearance of the system prompt from the default (A:\> or C:\>) to a user-defined prompt. Placing a PROMPT command in your AUTOEXEC.BAT file changes the prompt automatically when you boot DOS. If you enter PROMPT with no text, DOS goes back to the default prompt. The special codes may be entered using either uppercase or lowercase.

It is very helpful to know where you are on a hard disk as you switch from one directory to the next. The $p changes the system prompt to display the current directory. For example, the command **PROMPT PG** displays as **C:\DOS>** when the current directory is C:\DOS. Figure 7.2 shows the results of executing the four PROMPT commands shown in Examples of usage below.

Figure 7.2
Screen Display of
Changing Prompts

```
C:\DOS>PROMPT  Command?

Command?prompt  DATE = $d

DATE = Mon 01-17-1994prompt  Hi Babe $_$p$g

Hi Babe
C:\DOS>PROMPT

C>
```

Examples of usage:

C:\DOS> PROMPT Command?
(changes the system prompt from C:\DOS> to Command?)

C:\DOS> prompt DATE = $d
(changes the system prompt to display DATE = followed by the system date)

C:\DOS> prompt Hi Babe $_$p$g
(displays "Hi Babe" on the first system prompt line, followed by C:\DOS>
on the second line)

C:\DOS> PROMPT
(returns to the default system prompt)

TREE (Display Tree) Command (external)

Syntax: [d:][path]TREE [d:][path] [/F] [/A]

The **TREE** command displays all the directory paths on the specified drive.
Because TREE is an external command, the first [d:][path] in the syntax is the
path DOS needs to find it. It is not required if the directory containing DOS commands is included in the search path. The search path is created by the PATH
command. The second [d:][path] optionally specifies a disk and a directory to
display, rather than displaying the tree structure for the current directory.

When you are using the DOS shell, the directory tree is an integral part of the
shell. A graphical tree structure displays in the Directory Tree area. But the shell is
limited: it cannot be used to print out the tree structure like the TREE command.

When the **/F** option is used, TREE lists all the files in the root directory and all directories on the disk. The **/A** option is used whenever you have a printer that does not support graphic characters for drawing lines. Figure 7.3 shows a graphic display of a subdirectory structure.

Figure 7.3

Screen Display of Tree Structure Using TREE

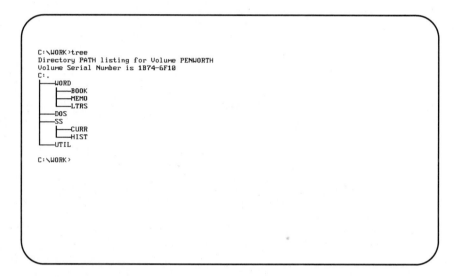

```
C:\WORK>tree
Directory PATH listing for Volume PENWORTH
Volume Serial Number is 1B74-6F10
C:.
├───WORD
│   ├───BOOK
│   ├───MEMO
│   └───LTRS
├───DOS
├───SS
│   ├───CURR
│   └───HIST
└───UTIL

C:\WORK>
```

Examples of usage:

C:\DOS> TREE /F
(displays all the files and directories in the current directory, which is the DOS directory on Drive C)

C:\DOS> TREE \WORD /F
(displays all files and directories in C:\WORD)

C:\> TREE >PRN
(prints a listing of all directories on Drive C)

C:\> tree /a >prn
(prints a listing of directories without using graphic characters)

HARD DISK MANAGEMENT TECHNIQUES

One difficult area of DOS to master is the effective control and management of files that accumulate on hard disks. Figure 7.4 provides an overview of many hard disk management techniques.

Figure 7.4
Hard Disk Management Techniques

- Develop good file naming conventions to help you better organize files.
- Use standard filename extentions to aid in classifying file types.
- Make backup copies of important data files regularly.
- Organize hard disk files into logical tree subdirectories.
- Place data files in a separate subdirectory from program files. This will shorten the time required to back up only your data files. Program files do not need to be backed up on a regular basis.
- Use AUTOEXEC.BAT and CONFIG.SYS files to customize your boot process.
- Limit your root directory files only to those used for booting, such as the COMMAND.COM, CONFIG.SYS, and AUTOEXEC.BAT files.
- Use the PATH command in an AUTOEXEC.BAT file to tell DOS where to look to find program files that are not in the current directory.
- Use the DIR command regularly to verify which files are in the current directory.
- Use DIR*. to display directory names in the current directory. Directory names do not have extensions.
- Use CD.. to change to the parent directory in the tree, one up from the current directory.
- Use SCANDISK (or CHKDSK /F) periodically to fix any lost allocation clusters on the disk.
- Use DEFRAG periodically to eliminate file fragmentation on your hard disk.
- Use MSAV periodically to locate and remove any computer virus from your system.
- Deleted any unnecessary backup (.BAK) and temporary (.TMP) files from your hard disk.
- If you have only one floppy drive, create a temporary directory on your hard disk to serve as a transfer area for copying files from one floppy disk to another.
- Use a backup power supply to ensure a good supply of power to your computer. This will minimize any physical damage to your hard disk and/or loss of data.

Chapter 7

REVIEW QUESTIONS

1. How are files organized on hard disks?
2. What is the significance of the term *current directory* in DOS?
3. How are subdirectory names identified by DOS?
4. What is a DOS path?
5. Why might you want to use short subdirectory names?
6. What do the single-dot and double-dot directory entries represent in DOS?
7. What command switches from the current directory to another directory?
8. How do you switch to the root directory?

9. Describe how a specific directory in the Directory Tree area of the DOS shell is expanded using a mouse.

10. How can identical filenames (e.g., FORMAT.COM) exist multiple times on the same hard disk?

11. What specific command creates a directory named DOS under the root directory if the current subdirectory is \UTIL?

12. What specific command creates a directory named DOS under the current directory?

13. How do you remove a directory from a disk using the RD command?

14. How are multiple directories specified in the PATH command?

15. When multiple directories are included in a search path, which one is searched first?

16. What command is used to view the current search path?

17. What command is used to rename directories? What are the limitations?

18. What command displays all directory names and their files on a disk? Give an example.

19. What does the command DELTREE \WORD do?

20. Define two limitations of the MOVE command.

Chapter 7

FLOPPY DISK LAB EXERCISES

Most of the following exercises can be executed within the DOS shell. Your instructor can decide which approach (the shell or command line) should be used to complete these exercises. A student's floppy disk is used in place of a hard disk for these exercises to keep the hard disk from being changed in a shared lab environment.

1. Use the following commands to make a hierarchy of directories on Drive B similar to Figure 7.1.

```
A:\> MD B:\DOS

A:\> MD B:\UTIL

A:\> MD B:\WORD

A:\> MD B:\WORD\BOOK

A:\> MD B:\WORD\MEMO
```

```
A:\> MD B:\WORD\LTRS

A:\> MD B:\SS

A:\> MD B:\SS\CURR

A:\> MD B:\SS\HIST
```

2. Copy a file currently residing in the root directory of Drive B to each of the nine directories created in Exercise 1 above.

```
Example: COPY B:READ.ME B:\WORD
```

3. Check out your new directory structure by entering:

```
A:\> DIR B:
```
(lists files and directories in the root directory)

```
A:\> DIR B:\WORD
```
(lists all files and directories in \WORD — the screen should look similar to Figure 7.5)

```
A:\> TREE B:/F
```
(lists all files and directories on Drive B — the hierarchy of directories should look similar to Figure 7.6)

Figure 7.5

Screen Display of Directories in \WORD

```
C:\DOS>dir b:\word

 Volume in drive B is SOUTHWORTH
 Volume Serial Number is 141B-13E4
 Directory of B:\WORD

.              <DIR>        01-17-94   1:21p
..             <DIR>        01-17-94   1:21p
BOOK           <DIR>        01-17-94   1:21p
LTRS           <DIR>        01-17-94   1:21p
MEMO           <DIR>        01-17-94   1:21p
READ     ME          223 01-17-94  12:35p
        6 file(s)             223 bytes
                          506,880 bytes free

C:\DOS>
```

Figure 7.6
TREE Structure of Drive B

Directory PATH listing for Volume SOUTHWORTH
Volume Serial Number is 141B-13E4

```
B:.
        COMMAND.COM
        READ.ME
        TEST.1
        TEST.3
        TEST.4
        TEST.ROF
    ─── DOS
            READ.ME
    ─── UTIL
            READ.ME
    ─── WORD
            READ.ME
        ─── BOOK
                READ.ME
        ─── MEMO
                READ.ME
        ─── LTRS
                READ.ME
    ─── SS
            READ.ME
        ─── CURR
                READ.ME
        ─── HIST
                READ.ME
```

4. Work in different directories:

`A:\> B:`
(change the default drive to B)

`B:\> CD\WORD\MEMO`
(make MEMO the current directory)

`B:\> DIR`
(view changes to the desired directory only)

`B:\> CD\`
(change back to the root directory)

`B:\> DIR`
(list all files and directories on the root directory of Drive B)

5. Delete the directory named HIST:

`B:\> DEL \SS\HIST\*.*`
(enter Y to delete all files from HIST)

`B:\> RD \SS\HIST`
(remove HIST directory)

`B:\> A:TREE B:`
(test the removal of HIST by running TREE, which is an external command on Drive A)

6. Set up a path to your DOS external commands:

`B:\> PATH A:`
(set path to include Drive A)

`B:\> TREE B:`
(test the path, noting that it will find TREE on Drive A after first searching Drive B)

7. Change the system prompt to display the current directory. Then change to several directories to see the effect:

`B:\> PROMPT $P$G`

`B:\> CD\WORD`

`B:\> CD\SS\CURR`

`B:\> CD..`

`B:\> CD\`

8. Create a directory, move several files to it, and view the new directory to verify the operation was successful:

`B:\> MD \SS\HIST`
(create the HIST directory)

`B:\> MOVE \SS\CURR\*.* \SS\HIST`
(move all files on \SS\CURR to \SS\HIST)

`B:\> DIR \SS\HIST`
(display the filenames on the HIST directory)

9. Use the DELTREE command to remove a "branch" in your directory tree:

`B:\> DELTREE \SS`
(remove all files and directories associated with \SS)

`B:\> TREE`
(list all directories on Drive B)

10. Bonus exercise (requires application of prior learning):

- Change the default disk to Drive B. Copy all the TEST files from the root directory of Drive B to the DOS directory on Drive B, created previously in this lab exercise.

- From the root directory of Drive B, create directory TEMP.

- Change to TEMP, copy all TEST files from B:\DOS to TEMP, and use the DIR command to verify the copy process. Use wildcard characters whenever possible to save keystrokes and minimize errors.

- Finally, remove the TEMP directory and change back to the A:\> prompt.

This completes the Chapter 7 floppy disk lab exercises. Remove your disk(s) when you are done.

Chapter 7

HARD DISK LAB EXERCISES

Most of the following exercises can be executed within the DOS shell. Your instructor can decide which approach (the shell or command line) should be used to complete these exercises.

1. Use the following commands to make a hierarchy of directories on Drive A similar to Figure 7.1.

```
C:\DOS> MD A:\DOS

C:\DOS> MD A:\UTIL

C:\DOS> MD A:\WORD

C:\DOS> MD A:\WORD\BOOK

C:\DOS> MD A:\WORD\MEMO

C:\DOS> MD A:\WORD\LTRS

C:\DOS> MD A:\SS

C:\DOS> MD A:\SS\CURR

C:\DOS> MD A:\SS\HIST
```

2. Copy a file currently residing in the root directory of Drive A to each of the nine directories created above.

   Example: `COPY A:READ.ME A:\WORD`

3. Check out your new directory structure by entering:

```
C:\DOS> DIR A:
```
(lists files and directories in the root directory)

```
C:\DOS> DIR A:\WORD
```
(lists all files and directories in \WORD — the screen should look similar to Figure 7.5)

`C:\DOS> TREE A:/F`
(lists all files and directories on Drive A — the hierarchy of directories should look similar to Figure 7.6)

4. Work in different directories:

`C:\DOS> A:`
(change the default drive to A)

`A:\> CD\WORD\MEMO`
(make MEMO the current directory)

`A:\> DIR`
(view changes to the desired directory only)

`A:\> CD\`
(change back to the root directory)

`A:\> DIR`
(list all files and directories on the root directory of Drive A)

5. Remove the directory named HIST:

`A:\> DEL \SS\HIST\*.*`
(enter Y to delete all files from HIST)

`A:\> RD \SS\HIST`
(remove HIST directory)

`A:\> C:\DOS\TREE A:`
(test the removal of HIST by running TREE, which is an external command on Drive C)

6. Set up a path to your DOS external commands:

`A:\> PATH C:\DOS`
(set path to include the DOS directory on Drive C)

`A:\> TREE`
(test the path, noting that it will find TREE on Drive C after first searching Drive A)

7. Change the system prompt to display the current directory. Then change to several directories to see the effect:

`A:\> PROMPT $P$G`

`A:\> CD\WORD`

`A:\> CD\SS\CURR`

`A:\> CD..`

`A:\> CD\`

8. Create a directory, move several files to it, and view the new directory to verify the operation was successful:

    `A:\> MD \SS\HIST`
    (create the HIST directory)

    `A:\> MOVE \SS\CURR\*.* \SS\HIST`
    (move all files on \SS\CURR to \SS\HIST)

    `A:\> DIR \SS\HIST`
    (display the filenames on the HIST directory)

9. Use the DELTREE command to remove a "branch" in your directory tree:

    `A:\> DELTREE \SS`
    (remove all files and directories associated with \SS)

    `A:\> TREE`
    (list all directories on Drive A)

10. Bonus exercise (requires application of prior learning):

    • Change the default disk to Drive A. Copy all the TEST files from the root directory of Drive A to the DOS directory on Drive A, created previously in this lab exercise.

    • From the root directory of Drive A, create directory TEMP.

    • Change to TEMP, copy all TEST files from A:\DOS to TEMP, and use the DIR command to verify the copy process. Use wildcard characters whenever possible to save keystrokes and minimize errors.

    • Finally, remove the TEMP directory and change back to the C:\DOS> prompt.

This completes the Chapter 7 hard disk lab exercises. Remove your data disk before you leave the computer.

FILE PROTECTION AND SECURITY

NEW FILE MANAGEMENT COMMANDS

    DEFRAG Command

    MSBACKUP Command

    MSAV Command

    SCANDISK Command

LEVELS OF DELETE PROTECTION

IMPROVING SECURITY WITH INVISIBLE CHARACTERS

WINDOWS-HOSTED UTILITIES

FILE PROTECTION AND SECURITY

Before DOS 6, many users purchased utility support programs to provide added levels of file protection and security. In DOS 6, Microsoft incorporated programs from two frequently purchased software packages, Norton Utilities and PC-Tools Deluxe. As a result, DOS 6 meets the protection requirements of most users. This chapter explains several new file protection and security commands. In addition, it covers the three levels of protection offered via the UNDELETE command, and shows how the <Alt255> character is used to hide files and directories.

NEW FILE MANAGEMENT COMMANDS

DOS 6 provides the following extremely useful external commands:

DEFRAG   Eliminates file fragmentation on a disk.

MSBACKUP Provides a friendly and powerful way to back up files.

MSAV   Detects and eliminates most computer viruses from your system.

SCANDISK   Detects and repairs many types of disk errors (Version 6.2).

DEFRAG Command

Syntax: DEFRAG [d:] [/U] [/F] [/SD] [/H]

The **DEFRAG** command reorganizes files on the specified disk, eliminating any file fragmentation to optimize disk performance. A file becomes fragmented when pieces of the file are stored in different tracks on a disk. Fragmented files take much longer for DOS to access because the read/write heads must move from one track to another. You should defragment files on a periodic basis (even weekly) depending on the amount of file changes that have occurred on a disk. You can execute DEFRAG differently by using a variety of options.

The **/U** option defragments files and rewrites them such that the disk may contain empty spaces between files. This is unsatisfactory. If the empty spaces on disk are too small, new files will be fragmented.

The **/F** option defragments files and rewrites files such that the disk will not contain any empty spaces between files. Although this option takes a little longer to execute than the /U option, the /F option is recommended.

The **/SD** option physically orders the files on the disk based on the date stamp. This option places all files in sequence by the date and time, oldest files first. Application programs and obsolete data files are often the oldest files on a disk and are least likely to change. This option reduces the time it takes to move files each time DEFRAG executes.

The **/H** option lets you physically move hidden files. With the other options, hidden files remain untouched by DEFRAG. Using the /H option lets you obtain the highest level of disk optimization.

When defragmenting your hard disk, use the following command options to provide the best results:

```
DEFRAG C: /F/SD/H
```

The first time you run the above command, it may take 15 minutes or more to optimize your hard disk. This is especially true if you have lots of file fragmentation. Each subsequent execution, however, will normally take only a few minutes. Use DEFRAG regularly to significantly reduce the time required to access disk files.

Note: DEFRAG will not work if any of the following conditions exist:

- You are currently running Windows (or any other multitasking system). You must close and exit Windows before executing DEFRAG.

- If the DOS task swapper (see Chapter 13) is running. You must close all active tasks and exit the DOS shell before executing DEFRAG.

- If the disk contains errors, such as lost allocation clusters.

To fix any disk errors, the SCANDISK (covered later) should be executed immediately prior to running DEFRAG. If you don't have Version 6.2 or higher, then use the CHKDSK /F command to fix your disk. Because DEFRAG was written for Norton Utilities, the disk information provided by DEFRAG differs significantly from that provided by CHKDSK. Figure 8.1 shows the major differences.

Figure 8.1
Differences Between CHKDSK and DEFRAG Statistics

	CHKDSK	DEFRAG
Hidden and user files are counted separately	Yes	No
The volume label is counted as a file	Yes	No
The root directory is counted as a directory	Yes	No

If you enter DEFRAG with no options, you can interactively select execution options from menus. The system automatically analyzes the files on your disk and recommends the appropriate options. Figure 8.2 shows a DEFRAG screen, displaying a pull-down options menu overlaying a graphical representation of the disk's fragmentation and free space.

Figure 8.2

DEFRAG Screen

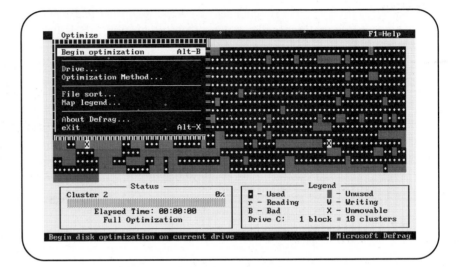

When you enter the **DEFRAG** command with no option specified, the defragmentation program first displays a list of drives on your computer. Use the arrow keys to highlight the disk to defragment and press the Enter key to select. The program then analyzes the selected disk and recommends a defragmentation option. Press the Enter key to start the process using the recommended options.

If you want to change the options, press the Tab key to highlight the Configure button and press the Enter key. The Optimize menu (Figure 8.2) displays so you can make the desired changes.

Examples of usage:

C:\DOS> DEFRAG /U
(defragments Drive C as quickly as possible, without reordering files and without eliminating empty spaces between files)

C:\DOS> DEFRAG /F /H
(defragments Drive C files, including hidden files, and eliminates all empty spaces between files)

C:\DOS> defrag b:/sd
(defragments Drive B files, reordering them such that the newest files created are physically written last)

C:\DOS> defrag
(executes the DEFRAG command and lets the system recommend options for defragmenting a disk)

C:\DOS> DEFRAG /?
(provides information about the defragment program)

MSBACKUP Command   Syntax: `MSBACKUP`

Without a backup facility, Microsoft claims that "it takes an average of 2,000 hours of work to replace all the data on an average hard disk." Microsoft's new backup program replaces the old, slow, and unwieldy BACKUP command included in previous DOS versions. Before DOS 6, if you wanted a more effective, easy-to-use facility for backing up your files, you had to purchase a separate backup program. The MSBACKUP command is very similar to the popular backup programs in Norton Utilities. Figure 8.3 shows the display screen when you load MSBACKUP from within DOS.

Figure 8.3
Display Screen
for MSBACKUP

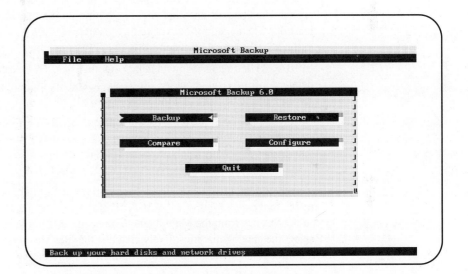

MSBACKUP includes extensive on-line help for commands, procedures, and dialog boxes. You can back up files to floppy disks in standard DOS format or in a compressed backup format. MSBACKUP can also format floppy disks as needed. The major levels of backup operations include the following:

- **Full backup** Backs up a selected group of files defined prior to running backup, such as by extension, directory, or disk drive. The Archive attribute is ignored with this level of backup.

- **Differential backup** Uses the Archive attribute to back up only files that have been changed or added since the last full backup. This level maintains only the latest versions of your files on a single set of backup disks. This approach is recommended if you often work with the same set of files.

- **Incremental backup** Uses the Archive attribute to back up only files that have been changed or added since your last full *or* previous incremental backup. Thus, this method may be more difficult to keep track of than the differential backup. Unless the last backup was a full backup, the incremental approach requires multiple sets of disks, one set for each incremental backup. If you do a full backup monthly and an incremental backup each week, a file that changes often could be included on each set of backup disks.

You should begin the backup process by fully backing up your files. Then, at regular intervals, make differential or incremental backups of your files. The first time you run MSBACKUP, you must define how backup will execute. These options are recorded in a system file named DEFAULT.SET. MSBACKUP uses floppy disk space to store backup-related files. Temporary work disks can be erased when backup is completed. In addition, to run backup you must have at least one file tagged for backup (e.g., the Archive attribute on). This attribute is automatically turned off when MSBACKUP saves a file.

MSBACKUP creates its own backup catalog files. These catalog files contain detailed information about the files you backed up, including the type of backup, the date of the backup, and the setup file used.

Once you have configured the backup process, MSBACKUP lets you save the specifications in a setup file. Suppose you created a setup file named MONTHLY.SET that defines a monthly full backup process on a group of files. To use this setup file in the future, you would enter **MSBACKUP MONTHLY**.

You should back up important files regularly. It isn't likely you will need to use the restore capabilities of MSBACKUP. If the need arises, run MSBACKUP and select Restore from the Main menu by pressing **R**. From a list of backup catalogs, select the catalog that most likely contains the files you need to restore. Follow the directions on the screen to highlight and restore the files.

Note: The MSBACKUP command files must be located on your hard disk; you cannot start MSBACKUP from a floppy disk. For more information on backup, use the **HELP MSBACKUP** command.

MSAV Command

Syntax: MSAV [d:] [/C] [/P]

In recent years, computer viruses have caused havoc among computer users. A computer virus is a nasty set of program instructions that attach themselves to an existing program file or the boot sector (track 0) of a disk. Many viruses try to disrupt your system by corrupting the boot sector of your hard disk. In addition, when a computer is infected, the virus may damage all files on the hard disk. Even if a trusted friend gives you a disk to try out, never use it to boot your system. This is the most common way viruses are spread among PCs. Instead, boot DOS normally and use an anti-virus program to ensure the disk is safe before using it.

The **MSAV** command runs a full-screen anti-virus utility program, which scans the specified disk for viruses and optionally removes them. MSAV is virtually identical to a popular anti-virus program, part of PC-Tools and written by Central Point Software. Because dozens of new viruses are being discovered each month, anti-virus programs must be updated periodically. Central Point Software is handling the updates for MSAV for a nominal fee. Figure 8.4 shows the MSAV screen menu with instructions to detect and remove viruses from the hard disk.

Figure 8.4
MSAV Screen

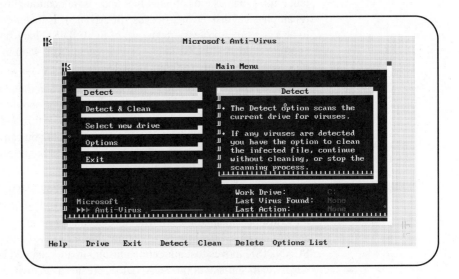

To help it work efficiently, MSAV automatically creates a file in each directory called CHKLIST.MS. A CHKLIST.MS file keeps track of previous file information, comparing it with new information to see if any files in the directory were changed (infected). **Note:** MSAV does not have an option to delete these files from your disk. Similar to DOSSHELL.INI, MSAV also creates a file in your DOS directory (MSAV.INI) to keep track of the options used the last time MSAV ran.

If you want to have the anti-virus utility program to "check and clean" Drive C each time you boot DOS, *without displaying the full-screen menu options*, include the following command in your AUTOEXEC.BAT file:

```
MSAV C: /C/P
```

The **/C** option detects and removes viruses from the specified drive. The **/P** option directs MSAV to execute without asking for any more execution options. For more information concerning the execution options, use the **HELP MSAV** command.

SCANDISK Command   Syntax: `SCANDISK [d:]`

DOS 6.2 includes **SCANDISK**, a new utility program that detects, diagnoses, and repairs disk errors. It is a big improvement over CHKDSK. In addition to file system errors, such as cross-linked files and lost allocation clusters, SCANDISK can repair physical disk errors. Because SCANDISK is menu-driven, you don't have to be a computer professional to use it! SCANDISK fixes both uncompressed and compressed disks (see Chapter 12). However, if you want to scan a compressed disk, you must supply the compressed volume name [d:].

If SCANDISK finds a problem, it displays an explanation of the problem, including what will happen when you fix it. Generally, you should select the Fix it option to let SCANDISK correct the problem for you. With this option, you can also have SCANDISK create an "Undo" floppy disk that you can later use to restore your disk to its previous state. For more information on the undo feature (and other options), use the **HELP SCANDISK** command.

Occasionally, you may get an error message that SCANDISK found some lost files or directories. Normally, you should select the Delete option to remove these lost or damaged files. If you have been experiencing disk problems, or you are just curious, select the Save option. Similar to the CHKDSK /F command, SCANDISK moves lost allocation clusters in a file named FILEnnnn.CHK, where nnnn starts at 0000. SCANDISK creates as many CHK files as it needs, one for each lost chain of clusters. You can view these files using the MORE command as follows:

```
MORE < FILE0000.CHK
```

When your curiosity is satisfied, you can delete the CHK files to free space on your disk. Sometimes, EDIT can be used to save any good parts of a CHK file as a different name before deleting the CHK file.

Figure 8.5
SCANDISK Operation

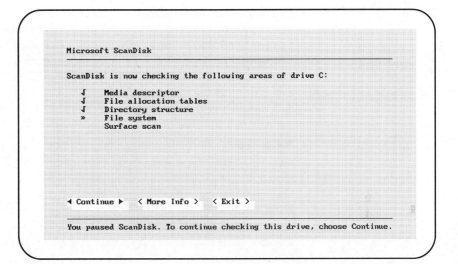

```
Microsoft ScanDisk

ScanDisk is now checking the following areas of drive C:
    √    Media descriptor
    √    File allocation tables
    √    Directory structure
    »    File system
         Surface scan




    ◄ Continue ►    ‹ More Info ›   ‹ Exit ›

You paused ScanDisk. To continue checking this drive, choose Continue.
```

Figure 8.5 shows the screen while SCANDISK is examining the disk for file system errors. This level of checking takes very little time. By default, when SCANDISK finishes checking for these errors, it asks if you want to do a surface scan. This process may take 10 minutes or more, depending on the size and speed of your hard disk. We recommend that you only exercise this option periodically (e.g., monthly), or whenever you are experiencing disk problems.

LEVELS OF DELETE PROTECTION

Once you delete a file from a disk, you won't always be able to recover it. Although the UNDELETE command can recover deleted files, it can only do so if a file's data has not been overwritten on the disk. In addition, it is possible that a deleted file remains unchanged on the disk, but subsequent changes to the directory or FAT prevent DOS from recovering the file. DOS 6 provides the following levels of protection to assist in the recovery of files deleted accidentally:

- **Standard** The lowest and default level of protection. It requires neither additional memory nor disk space, but still makes it possible to recover many deleted files with the UNDELETE command. UNDELETE was first available with DOS 5. For the Standard level of protection to be truly effective, you should undelete files as soon as possible. If you work with the DOS Shell (or Windows) free disk space is frequently used by temporary swap files. This requires a higher level of protection than Standard. **Note:** Beginning with Version 6.2, UNDELETE can recover deleted directories.

- **Delete Tracker** An intermediate level of protection. Available with DOS 5, it requires a small amount of memory (13.5KB) and additional disk space. Delete Tracker will use up to 14MB (1.2%) on a 120MB hard disk. When freeing up space in the FAT for deleted files, it saves the old FAT and directory information in a hidden tracking file (PCTRACKER.DEL). Delete Tracker can recover deleted files when the data remains on the disk but access to the data was destroyed on the current directory and/or FAT. Delete Tracker is activated by executing the UNDELETE command with the **/T** option.

- **Delete Sentry** The highest level of protection. It requires a small amount of memory and more disk space than Delete Tracker. Delete Sentry is new to DOS 6. It uses a hidden directory named SENTRY to save a duplicate copy of files when they are deleted. This technique gives files a very good chance of being successfully recovered long after being deleted. The number of deleted files saved is limited to about 7% of your total hard disk space. When more disk space is needed, DOS purges the oldest files until enough space has been freed to accommodate newly deleted files. A file named UNDELETE.INI saves the execution options used the last time Delete Sentry ran. This file can be edited (see Chapter 10) to direct DOS how to purge files from the SENTRY directory. Delete Sentry is loaded by executing the UNDELETE command with the **/S** option. Figure 8.6 shows the initial display screen for Delete Sentry.

Figure 8.6
Delete Sentry Screen

```
C:\DOS>undelete /s

UNDELETE - A delete protection facility
Copyright (C) 1987-1993 Central Point Software, Inc.
All rights reserved.

UNDELETE loaded.

Delete Protection Method is Delete Sentry.
Enabled for drives : C


C:\DOS>
```

If you use either Delete Tracker or Delete Sentry, you should include the UNDELETE command (with /T or /S) in your AUTOEXEC.BAT file. This will ensure a consistent level of deletion protection is used each time you boot your system.

When you use Delete Sentry, available disk space is reported differently by DIR and CHKDSK. The DIR command treats the SENTRY directory as occupying zero bytes, because that space could be used if required. However, the CHKDSK command reports space based on units allocated in the FAT. CHKDSK includes the actual space used by the SENTRY directory. For more information on Delete Tracker and Delete Sentry, use the on-line help facility to view the specific notes for the UNDELETE command.

IMPROVING SECURITY WITH INVISIBLE CHARACTERS

When office computers are shared, it may be prudent to protect data from co-workers. Here is a simple way to keep others from accessing a directory on your hard disk that contains sensitive information.

DOS has an invisible character that is created by holding down the Alt key while entering 255 from the numeric keypad. The ASCII 255 character can be used as the last character of a directory name, such as PERS<Alt255>. Because this directory name displays as PERS, no one can change to that directory without knowing how to enter the invisible character. Thus, all files on that directory are protected.

Besides providing security from the command line, this technique is effective against potential intruders who use the DOS Shell or Windows. Because the system is unable to interpret the directory name completely, the <Alt255> character prevents someone from opening, viewing, or deleting the contents of the directory.

WINDOWS-HOSTED UTILITIES

Because many PCs are running Windows, Microsoft includes three Windows programs which can be executed within Windows, without having to exit to DOS.

- **MWBACKUP** The Windows version of MSBACKUP used to back up files. Other than some cosmetic differences in the display screens, the two versions are very similar.

- **MWAV** The Windows version of MSAV, an anti-virus facility. It is similar to MSAV with two exceptions: (1) it cannot be used with the options discussed earlier, and (2) it includes an option to delete all the CHKLIST.MS files from a drive.

- **MWUNDEL** The Windows version of UNDELETE to undelete files. The Windows version includes one additional capability: it lists all deleted files along with the probable chances of recovery for each file.

When you install DOS 6 with the Windows versions of these facilities, DOS places the program icons in a program group called Microsoft Tools. Figure 8.7 shows the Microsoft Tools group window. As a Windows user, you no longer need to exit Windows to back up, recover files, or scan for viruses. However, we recommend you don't install the Windows version of MSBACKUP. If the files needed to load Windows are bad, you can't restore them using the Windows version; you must use the DOS version.

Figure 8.7
Microsoft Tools
Group Window

If you initially installed DOS 6 without the Windows versions, you can use the SETUP command with the /E option to add features later on.

Chapter 8

REVIEW QUESTIONS

1. What is a fragmented file and how does fragmentation occur?
2. What is the primary difference between the /U and /F options of DEFRAG?
3. Why would it be more efficient in the long run to run DEFRAG with the /F option?
4. Why should you run DEFRAG regularly?
5. Why must you fix any file disk errors before running DEFRAG?
6. Why do you think it is important to have a backup program that is easy to use?
7. What is a full backup?
8. How does a differential backup differ from an incremental one?
9. How does MSBACKUP use the Archive attribute?
10. How do you define a custom setup for MSBACKUP?
11. What is a computer virus and how is it spread?
12. How can you detect and eliminate a virus from your computer?

13. What is the purpose of the CHKLIST.MS file?

14. In what way does SCANDISK do a better job of fixing disks than CHKDSK?

15. What would be the benefit of viewing data in a file with a CHK extension?

16. What command lets you quickly view the contents of FILE0003.CHK?

17. In what way, and at what cost, does Delete Tracker provide better undelete capability than the standard level of delete protection?

18. In what way, and at what cost, does Delete Sentry provide better undelete capability than Delete Tracker?

19. How does the <Alt255> character make filenames and directory names "invisible" to the user?

20. As a Windows user, why might you decide not to install MWBACKUP?

Chapter 8

LAB EXERCISES

For both floppy and hard disk systems

Due to the different processing environments that students in a lab setting operate, these exercises are designed to work with a floppy disk (Drive A). Be sure to get permission from your instructor before doing these exercises with the hard disk (Drive C).

1. Use the HELP command to view information related to the three commands you will experiment with in these exercises: DEFRAG, MSAV, and SCANDISK.

2. Use the DEFRAG command to defragment the floppy disk in Drive A. It is unlikely that you will have much (if any) fragmentation, but it may be beneficial for you to see how DEFRAG operates. To defragment the disk in Drive A, without specifying a reordering sequence, enter **DEFRAG A:/F**.

   If the disk in Drive A has no fragmentation, DEFRAG ends rather quickly, beeping cheerfully as it returns you to the system prompt.

3. Use the MSAV command to see if the disk in Drive A has any computer viruses by entering **MSAV A:**. If MSAV detects a virus, notify your instructor immediately.

4. Although it is unlikely you will have any disk errors on the floppy disk in Drive A, use the following command to locate and repair any errors: **SCANDISK A:**. If you don't have Version 6.2 (or higher), use the **CHKDSK /F** command instead.

   If any lost data was found, follow the directions displayed on the screen for saving a CHK file. Then, use the **MORE** command to show your instructor the lost data in the CHK file(s).

This completes the Chapter 8 lab exercises. Remove your disk(s) before you leave the computer.

THREE IMPORTANT CONCEPTS

REDIRECTION

PIPING WITH FILTERS

    SORT Command

    MORE Command

    FIND Command

COMMAND LINE EDITING

    DOS Editing Keys

    DOSKEY Command

Chapter 9

THREE IMPORTANT CONCEPTS

This chapter presents three DOS concepts that will be very helpful to you. The first concept is redirection, which is a technique used for changing the standard input or output device of a DOS command, thereby adding flexibility to your commands. Closely related to redirection is piping, a method of transferring the output of one command as input to another. Piping lets you combine DOS commands to form a more powerful command. Special-purpose commands known as filters are used with redirection and piping. Filters modify portions of the information that passes through them. DOS has three filters: SORT, MORE, and FIND. Command line editing, the last important concept, lets you make changes to a previously entered command without having to retype the entire command.

REDIRECTION

Redirection changes the standard output device used by a DOS command to another output device. It can also redirect the standard input device. The standard input device is the keyboard and the standard output device is the display screen. The less than sign (<) defines a new source of input and the greater than sign (>) defines a new target of output. In the examples that follow, the first > is part of the system prompt (i.e., A:\>). Because the redirection sign is also a delimiter, a space is *not* required before or after the redirection sign in the command line. We have included a space in some examples to improve readability.

Examples of usage:

    A:\> DIR >B:DIR.LST
(redirects the standard DIR display from the screen to a file on Drive B named DIR.LST)

    A:\> dir>prn
(directs the DIR display to go to the printer)

    A:\> CHKDSK > PRN
(redirects the displayed output to the printer)

    A:\> Sort < B:filea.txt > B:fileb.txt
(uses FILEA.TXT as the input for a SORT command, or filter, that redirects the sorted results to FILEB.TXT)

PIPING WITH FILTERS

Piping uses the output from one DOS command as the input for another DOS command. DOS transfers (pipes) data by creating a temporary work file on the default disk. Thus, the default disk cannot be full or write-protected. The first command outputs to a piping file, used as input by the second command. Multiple pipes can be used in a single command line. When the final operation is completed, DOS deletes all temporary pipe files. You can think of piping as a form of redirection. With piping, however, the temporary files are created and deleted by DOS rather than by the user.

Piping usually involves DOS commands called filters. **Filters** receive data, do something with it, and pass it to the next step. The DOS commands most often used with piping are:

SORT Sorts a text file into a desired sequence, writing the results on the screen. It does not distinguish between uppercase and lowercase letters.

MORE Displays only one screen of output at a time, pausing to let the user press any key to continue. In effect, it gives the /P option (used with DIR) to any DOS command that displays its output on the screen.

FIND Searches a file for a specific string of text, displaying any lines of text that contain the desired string.

Because filters are external DOS commands, a disk drive designator is required when they are not on the default disk. To specify a piping operation, DOS uses the broken vertical bar (|), normally located on top of the \ key. Like the redirection symbol, the piping symbol is also a delimiter. The standard output device for the TYPE and SORT commands is the monitor. If you pipe the output from TYPE into a SORT command, the monitor displays the sorted listing of the file in ascending sequence. For example:

```
A:\> TYPE PHONE.LST | SORT
```

If your PHONE.LST contained names of friends with their phone numbers, this command would display them in name sequence. The above example is equivalent to the following set of commands:

```
TYPE PHONE.LST > A:TEMPFILE
SORT < A:TEMPFILE
DEL A:TEMPFILE
```

SORT Command (external)

SORT arranges data according to an industry standard using each character's ASCII value. The default sequence places lines of data in ascending order as follows:

1. Spaces come first.

2. Most of the special characters come next.

3. Numeric characters (0–9) are sequenced next.

4. Alphabetic characters come last.

To reverse the order of a sort, include the reverse option (**/R**). The following command produces a listing in descending order:

```
A:\> TYPE PHONE.LST | SORT /R
```

**MORE Command
(external)**

If you find that a sorted listing is too large to fit on a single screen, you can pipe it to the **MORE** command. Figure 9.1 shows what the first page might look like when the following command is executed. Notice how the piping symbol is also used as a delimiter.

```
A:\> TYPE PHONE.LST|SORT|MORE
```

**Figure 9.1
Screen Display of
Sorted PHONE.LST**

```
ALLISON, EDWARD        634-1114
ALLISON, JERRY         635-7711
ALLISON, JIM           634-0055
ALLISON, MOLLY         634-0111
ALLISON, SUSAN         634-2341
ANDERSON, ANNA         634-6003
ANDERSON, DAVID        635-0089
ANDERSON, HARRY        634-0123
ANDERSON, SUSAN        634-7539
ANDERSON, WALLY        635-9016
ATWATER, KELLY         635-9962
BAKER, RICHARD         635-8009
FRANKLIN, BENJAMIN     635-6388
FRANKLIN, EDWARD       635-8902
FRANKLIN, FRANCES      635-9154
FRANKLIN, PENNY        635-2284
GAPEN, ANN             635-8442
JENSON, JOSEPH         634-2276
JENSON, SUZI           635-9022
SAMPSON, DAVID         634-7861
SAMPSON, SUSAN         635-8873
WATSON, EDWARD         635-4567
-- More --
```

**FIND Command
(external)**

The **FIND** command searches a file for a given string of characters. It locates all lines from the specified file that contain the desired text. Text must be enclosed in a set of double quotation marks and must use the correct uppercase and lowercase. For example, suppose PHONE.LST contained uppercase names and phone numbers. To display the phone number for everyone named Susan, enter:

```
A:\> TYPE PHONE.LST | FIND "SUSAN"
```

However, FIND would *not* locate any records in the following example because PHONE.LST has no lowercase characters.

```
A:\> TYPE PHONE.LST | FIND "Susan"
```

Figure 9.2 shows what the screen might look like after the last two piping commands were executed.

Figure 9.2
Screen Display of FIND

```
A>TYPE PHONE.LST | FIND "SUSAN"
ALLISON, SUSAN          634-2341
ANDERSON, SUSAN         634-7539
WILSON, SUSAN           635-7921
WATSON, SUSAN           634-5530
SAMPSON, SUSAN          635-8873

A>TYPE PHONE.LST | FIND "Susan"

A>
```

The FIND command can be used with any file or ASCII listing, such as the output of a DIR listing. To display a directory of just the files that were created (or changed) on November 16, 1994, enter the following command:

```
A:\> DIR | FIND "11-16-94"
```

Using filters can give you the ability to create your own commands. For example, suppose you wanted to display all the files on Drive C with an extension of BAK, one screen at a time. You could "create" your own new command as follows:

```
C:\DOS> CHKDSK /V | FIND ".BAK" | MORE
```

Piping and redirection may be combined in a single operation. To have a sorted directory listing saved to an ASCII file called B:SORTED.TXT, you could enter the following:

```
A:\> DIR|SORT>B:SORTED.TXT
```

Sometimes it is useful to display data from a listable file on the screen, one screen at a time. If ACCOUNT.TXT was a large file on Drive B, you could enter:

```
A:\> MORE < B:ACCOUNT.TXT
```

This directs MORE to get its input from B:ACCOUNT.TXT. MORE displays its output on the monitor one screen at a time. You could have obtained the same result with piping by entering:

```
A:\> TYPE B:ACCOUNT.TXT | MORE
```

In this case, redirection is more efficient than piping because it does not have to create and delete a temporary piping file.

COMMAND LINE EDITING

There will be times you want to execute a previous DOS command, exactly as you entered it earlier, or with some minor change. DOS keeps track of the commands you enter, letting you recall them on a selective basis. Once the command is recalled, you can change it before you press the Enter key to execute it. DOS supports this process, called **command line editing**, in two ways: with DOS editing keys and with the DOSKEY command.

DOS Editing Keys

Sometimes you need to make minor changes to the last DOS command entered. Instead of keying the command line again, you can use the **DOS editing keys** to recall it and modify just the characters that need changing.

When you enter a command, DOS puts a copy of it in a temporary storage location called an input buffer. You can recall the last command from the buffer and make changes without duplicating keystrokes. The process of editing involves inserting and deleting characters in the command line. Figure 9.3 summarizes the DOS editing keys used most often.

Figure 9.3
DOS Editing Keys

<F1>   Displays one character at a time from the buffer.

<F3>   Displays all characters in the buffer (or the rest of the buffer).

<Ins>   Inserts one or more characters in the buffer at the cursor location.

<Del>   Deletes one character at a time from the buffer.

The best way to understand how to use the DOS editing keys is to try them. The three exercises that follow show how to use the editing keys and will help reinforce what you have learned.

1. Suppose you entered **COPY A:TEST1.XT A:TEST1.BAK** and were given an error message because TEST1.XT was not found on Drive A (assume it should have been TEST1.TXT). To correct the command with the editing keys:

   • Press <F1> until the X is next to be retrieved, displaying COPY A:TEST1.

   • Press <Ins> and then press the letter **T**.

   • Press <F3> to display the rest of the buffer. Now it should show
     COPY A:TEST1.TXT A:TEST1.BAK

   • Press the enter key to execute the command and return to the system prompt. It is normal to get an error message at this point because the file TEST1.TXT does not exist on Drive A.

2. Suppose you entered **COPY A:TEST3.DOC A:TEST.BAK** and wanted to

redo it because you meant to copy to A:TEST3.BAK. To correct the error:

- Press <F3> to display all characters in the input buffer.
- Use the Backspace key to delete the last four characters (.BAK).
- Type **3.BAK** and press the Enter key.

3. Suppose you entered **TYPE A:TEST3.DOC** and got what you wanted, but now you also want to display A:TEST2.DOC.

- Press <F1> until the 3 in the filename is the next to be displayed.
- Press 2 to replace the next character (the 3) in the buffer.
- Press <F3> to finish displaying the buffer and then press the Enter key.

DOSKEY Command (external)

The DOS editing keys can recall and modify only the last command entered. **DOSKEY** can recall and edit previously entered commands. It uses a special buffer area (512 bytes) to record the last 48 commands. However, DOSKEY must be executed before it can start saving commands. It is called a **Terminate-and-Stay-Resident (TSR)** program because it stays in RAM until you turn off the system or reboot DOS. To install DOSKEY, enter **DOSKEY** at the system prompt. **Note:** Chapter 13 shows how to load DOSKEY so it does not take up valuable space needed by application programs.

To work with a previous command from the buffer, use the Up arrow key to find the desired command. If you go back too far, use the Down arrow key to go forward. Use the PgUp and PgDn keys to recall the first and last commands in the buffer. For example, let us assume that you have just entered the following commands:

```
DOSKEY
DIR B:
DBASE
COPY B:TESTFILE.DOC A:*.BAK
DIR A: /W
```

To recall the COPY command to execute it again with minor changes, press the Up arrow key twice — once for the last command entered (DIR), and a second time to recall the COPY command. DOSKEY editing keys can be used to make minor changes to the current command line. Figure 9.4 lists the DOSKEY editing keys and their functions within a command line.

Figure 9.4
DOSKEY Editing Keys

Left arrow	Moves the cursor back one character.
Right arrow	Moves the cursor forward one character.
HOME key	Moves the cursor to the beginning of the command line.
END key	Moves the cursor to the end of the command line.
Ins key	Toggles the insert mode on or off.
Del key	Deletes the character at the location of the cursor.
Esc key	Cancels editing, leaving the command line unchanged.

Chapter 9

REVIEW QUESTIONS

1. What is the standard input device in DOS?

2. What is the standard output device in DOS?

3. How would you use redirection to print a directory listing?

4. What is a piping file and how is it used?

5. What type of files are sorted by the SORT command?

6. What does the /R option do when added to the SORT command?

7. What is the purpose of the MORE filter?

8. What is displayed with the command **DIR | FIND "CONFIG"** ?

9. What command displays A:README.TXT a screen at a time?

10. What two different commands may be entered to print the contents of A:README.TXT?

11. What command is entered to view just the displayed number of files in a directory listing? Hint: Use a unique string of characters like "(s)".

12. What two methods can be used to edit the DOS command line?

13. When are DOS editing keys used?

14. What DOS editing key displays all the characters in the buffer?

15. How are characters deleted from the input buffer of a command line?

16. What is the primary use for the DOSKEY command?

17. Assuming DOSKEY is installed and you have entered several DOS commands, where will the cursor be after you press the Up arrow key followed by the HOME key?

18. What will the command **CHKDSK /V | SORT > PRN** accomplish?

19. Once you start changing a command line with the DOS editing keys, how can you abort the process and leave the command line unchanged?

20. Why does DOSKEY need to remain in RAM when executed?

FLOPPY DISK LAB EXERCISES

These exercises should all be done from the system prompt.

1. For this exercise, you will be creating some temporary files on the DOS disk. Therefore, you should remove any write-protect tab on the DOS disk. Boot DOS (Drive A) and insert your data disk in Drive B. Enter **DIR B:** and experiment with redirection and piping as follows:

DIR > B:TEST1.DIR
(redirects the directory from the monitor to a file named TEST1.DIR)

SORT < B:TEST1.DIR > B:TEST2.DIR
(sorts the previous file and redirects it to another filename)

TYPE B:TEST2.DIR | MORE
(displays the sorted directory listing)

DIR | SORT > B:TEST3.DIR
(outputs the sorted directory to a file)

TYPE B:TEST3.DIR | MORE
(displays a file, one screen at a time)

DIR /OS | MORE
(lists the directory of the default disk ordered by file size)

DIR B:/O-S
(lists a directory of Drive B ordered by descending file size — the screen should look similar to Figure 9.5)

Figure 9.5
Screen Display of Sorted Directory

```
C:\DOS>dir b:/o-s

 Volume in drive B is SOUTHWORTH
 Volume Serial Number is 141B-13E4
 Directory of B:\

COMMAND  COM        ·54,619 09-30-93   6:20a
TEST1    DIR          4,637 01-17-94   2:40p
TEST2    DIR          4,637 01-17-94   2:40p
TEST3    DIR          4,637 01-17-94   2:41p
READ     ME             223 01-17-94  12:35p
TEST     1              223 01-17-94  12:35p
TEST     3              223 01-17-94  12:35p
TEST     4              223 01-17-94  12:35p
TEST     ROF            223 01-17-94  12:35p
DOS          <DIR>          01-17-94   1:20p
UTIL         <DIR>          01-17-94   1:21p
WORD         <DIR>          01-17-94   1:21p
        12 file(s)        69,645 bytes
                         497,664 bytes free

C:\DOS>
```

2. If you are connected to a printer, you can complete this portion of the lab exercise. Otherwise, just read it. To print a sorted directory listing by file size on the printer, enter: **DIR/OS > PRN**

   To print a sorted directory of just those files on Drive B with a filename containing "TEST" on the printer, enter the following:

   DIR B: | FIND "TEST" | SORT > PRN

3. Install the DOSKEY command by entering **DOSKEY** at the system prompt. If DOSKEY cannot be installed, ask your instructor for help.

4. Experiment with DOS editing keys by entering the following:

   ```
   DIR A:
   ```
   (press the Enter key to execute this command)

   ```
   DIR A: /P
   ```
   (use F3 to allow you to easily add /P)

   ```
   COPY B:TEST3.DR B:TEST3.BAK
   ```
   (forces the message, "File not found")

   ```
   COPY B:TEST3.DIR B:TEST3.BAK
   ```
   (use the DOS editing keys to correct the previous entry)

5. If DOSKEY is installed (see Exercise 3), recall the last few commands you entered by pressing the Up arrow key. You can scroll down through the list by using the Down arrow key. When you locate the command that resulted in a directory listing of Drive A with the pause option, add the /OE option to it and press the Enter key to get the directory in extension sequence.

6. Bonus exercise (requires application of prior learning):

   • Enter: **SORT < B:READ.ME > B:READ.SRT** to create a new file, the sorted equivalent of the READ.ME file on Drive B. Use the TYPE command to display it on the screen. Notice that complete lines of text were sorted, not each word (see Figure 9.6).

Figure 9.6
Screen Display of
READ.SRT

```
C:\DOS>sort < b:read.me >b:read.srt

C:\DOS>type b:read.srt
either a space or a comma.  They can be used interchangeably
must be separated by delimiters.  Delimiters are normally
When entering DOS commands, the commands and parameters
within any command (i.e., COPY A:OLDFILE,B:).

C:\DOS>
```

- Enter: **TYPE B:READ.ME | FIND "comma"** to display only those lines in the file containing the string "comma". Repeat this operation using "comma". How did adding a space to the FIND string affect the output?

This completes the Chapter 9 floppy disk lab exercises. Remove your disk(s) before you leave the computer.

Chapter 9

HARD DISK LAB EXERCISES

These exercises should all be done from the system prompt.

1. Boot DOS (Drive C) and insert your data disk in Drive A. Make sure you are at the DOS portion of the hard disk before proceeding. Enter **DIR A:** and experiment with redirection and piping as follows:

   DIR > A:TEST1.DIR
   (redirects the directory from the monitor to a file named TEST1.DIR)

   SORT < A:TEST1.DIR > A:TEST2.DIR
   (sorts the previous file and redirects it to another filename)

   TYPE A:TEST2.DIR | MORE
   (displays the sorted directory listing)

   DIR | SORT > A:TEST3.DIR
   (outputs the sorted directory to a file)

TYPE A:TEST3.DIR | MORE
(displays a file, one screen at a time)

DIR /OS | MORE
(lists the directory of the default disk ordered by file size)

DIR A:/O-S
(lists a directory of Drive A ordered by descending file size — the screen should look similar to Figure 9.5)

2. If you are connected to a printer, you can complete this portion of the lab exercise. Otherwise, just read it. To print a sorted directory listing by file size on the printer, enter: **DIR/OS > PRN**

   To print a sorted directory of just those filenames on Drive A with a filename containing "TEST" on the printer, enter the following:

   ```
   DIR A: | FIND "TEST" | SORT > PRN
   ```

3. Install the DOSKEY command by entering **DOSKEY** at the system prompt. If DOSKEY cannot be installed, ask your instructor for help.

4. Experiment with DOS editing keys by entering the following:

   ```
   DIR
   ```
   (press the Enter key to execute this command)

   ```
   DIR /P
   ```
   (use F3 to allow you to easily add /P)

   ```
   COPY A:TEST3.DR A:TEST3.BAK
   ```
   (forces the message, "File not found")

   ```
   COPY A:TEST3.DIR A:TEST3.BAK
   ```
   (use the DOS editing keys to correct the previous entry)

5. If DOSKEY is installed (see Exercise 3), recall the last few commands you entered by pressing the Up arrow key. You can scroll down through the list by using the Down arrow key. When you locate the command that resulted in a directory listing with the pause option, add the /OE option to it and press the Enter key to get the directory in extension sequence.

6. Bonus exercise (requires application of prior learning):

   • Enter: **SORT < A:READ.ME > A:READ.SRT** to create a new file, the sorted equivalent of the READ.ME file on Drive A. Use the TYPE command to display it on the screen. Notice that complete lines of text were sorted, not each word (see Figure 9.6).

   • Enter: **TYPE A:READ.ME | FIND "comma"** to display only those lines in the file containing the string "comma". Repeat this operation using "comma". How did adding a space to the FIND string affect the output?

This completes the Chapter 9 hard disk lab exercises. Remove your data disk before you leave the computer.

INTRODUCTION TO BATCH FILES

INTRODUCTION TO BATCH FILES

Thus far you learned how to execute DOS commands by entering them one after another at the system prompt. A **batch file** is a group of commands that the computer automatically executes as a set, instead of one at a time. This text file has an extension of BAT and contains an entire "batch" of commands. DOS's ability to create and run batch files is a powerful feature. All its commands execute in sequence without intervention, freeing you to do other things while the computer does all the work. The primary objectives of this chapter are for you:

- To understand how batch files work, including the AUTOEXEC.BAT file.
- To see how replaceable parameters add flexibility to batch files.
- To learn how to use the REM, PAUSE, and ECHO batch file commands.
- To learn how to use the full-screen text editor (EDIT) to create and modify batch files.

THE AUTOEXEC.BAT FILE

To execute a command each time DOS starts, the command must be placed in a special batch file called **AUTOEXEC.BAT**, appropriately named for AUTOmatic EXECution. This is especially useful with hard disk systems that use the PROMPT and PATH commands. Other commands used during the boot process are covered later.

Immediately after DOS boots, the system searches for an AUTOEXEC.BAT file in the root directory of the system disk. If the file is found, DOS executes any commands contained in AUTOEXEC.BAT, bypassing the automatic prompting for DATE and TIME. If you do not have a battery-powered clock-calendar in your computer, you must include DATE and TIME commands in your AUTOEXEC.BAT file. Otherwise, you can let DOS automatically set the system date and time from your clock-calendar. If you have a hard disk system, you most likely have an AUTOEXEC.BAT file already—so don't change it or delete it accidentally.

Suppose you were setting up an office accounting system that required a specific set of tasks to be done whenever the system boots. You could use an AUTOEXEC.BAT file containing the specific commands you require. It could look similar to Figure 10.1.

Figure 10.1
Sample AUTOEXEC.BAT File

```
PATH C:\DOS;C:\UTIL;C:\MENU
PROMPT $P$G
SET DIRCMD=/ON
SET TEMP=C:\DOS
DEL C:\DOS\*.TMP
COPY C:\SSFILES\BUDGET.WK1 A:BUDGET.BAK
CD C:\SS
LOTUS
```

The computer automatically executes these commands each time the system is turned on. This AUTOEXEC.BAT file assumes that the system date and time are automatically updated from a hardware clock-calendar. It executes the following tasks each time DOS boots:

- Sets the default search path to use C:\DOS, C:\UTIL, and C:\MENU.
- Causes the system prompt to display the current disk and directory.
- Sets the default for directory listings to be in filename sequence.
- Sets C:\DOS as the default directory for any temporary files created by DOS or application programs.
- Deletes any temporary files on the DOS directory.
- Copies a file in the SSFILES directory of the hard disk to Drive A.
- Changes to the SS directory on the hard disk.
- Executes an application program called LOTUS.

This approach can simplify and standardize the startup procedures for any system. A batch file may be as simple or as complex as you want it to be. It keeps you from the tedious task of entering a group of commands each time. In addition, it lets you relax while the computer works for you!

CREATING BATCH FILES

Suppose you didn't want to enter CHKDSK every time you asked DOS to check a disk. You could create a simple batch file called CK.BAT that lets you execute the CHKDSK command by entering **CK**, the batch file name. Whenever you enter the name of an external command, such as FORMAT or CHKDSK, DOS searches for it on the specified disk. If it is found, DOS executes the command. Executing a batch file works in much the same way. You must enter the batch file name to allow DOS to find and execute the batch file. When you enter a DOS command or a batch file command, the system looks for a command to execute in the current directory. It first looks for a COM file with that name. If a COM file is not found, DOS looks for an EXE file and then a BAT file. Normally, you should name batch files with a different filename from COM or EXE files. Otherwise, the DOS command with that name may be found and executed before the batch file is found.

Because you already know how to use the COPY CON command, use it to create a batch file from the keyboard (CONsole) as shown below. Press the Enter key after each line is typed. Always press the F6 function key <F6> and then the Enter key at the end of the last line of text to exit the COPY CON operation.

```
A:\> COPY CON CK.BAT <Enter>
      CHKDSK <F6> <Enter>
```

From now on, when you want to execute CHKDSK, you only need to enter **CK** to execute this batch file. However, CK.BAT is only able to execute CHKDSK for Drive A (the default drive). What if you want to check another drive?

USING REPLACEABLE PARAMETERS

Many DOS commands require parameters that vary each time you enter the command. Batch file features called **replaceable parameters** let you substitute variable data into batch files. Batch files use a special code (%n) that lets variable data substitute in its place. You may need more than one variable parameter in batch files. A number (1–9) follows the percent sign (%), giving you nine different variables (replaceable parameters) that may be substituted in a batch file.

The batch file above (CK.BAT) could include a single replaceable parameter (%1) that lets you specify a disk drive when you execute the batch file. Redo the COPY CON command above, and change the command CHKDSK (in the batch file) to **CHKDSK %1**. Then, when the batch file executes, the disk drive must be included as a parameter. The disk drive substitutes for the %1 entry in the batch file. For example, you could enter **CK B:** to display a CHKDSK status report for Drive B. The value B: substitutes for %1 in the batch file. Likewise, **CK A:** executes the CHKDSK command for Drive A.

Although earlier versions of DOS didn't have a move command, the batch file capability let you create your own command to move files. The following sample batch file (**MOV.BAT**) moves a file from one location to another. It contains two commands and two replaceable parameters.

```
COPY %1 %2
DEL %1
```

This batch file looks more complicated than the previous example because it contains two replaceable parameters. Each replaceable parameter in the batch file is replaced by the appropriate value when the batch file executes. For example, %1 represents the filename to be moved, and %2 represents the location of the moved file.

A batch file is executed by entering the batch file name with any required parameters. Each parameter must be typed in the correct order, such as the values for %1, then %2, and so on. Suppose you wanted to use this new batch file to move BUDGET.TXT on Drive A to Drive B. To execute MOV.BAT, enter:

```
A:\> MOV BUDGET.TXT B:
```

The two parameters supplied during execution of the batch file (BUDGET.TXT and B:) substitute for the replaceable parameters (%1 and %2) in the batch file. In effect, the execution of this batch file is identical to entering the following two commands:

```
A:\> COPY BUDGET.TXT B:
A:\> DEL BUDGET.TXT
```

BATCH FILE COMMANDS

All batch file commands are internal DOS commands. They give added power to batch file processing. This chapter introduces you to three batch file commands:

REM Provides for remarks in batch files.

PAUSE Pauses to allow operator input into a batch file.

ECHO Sets the batch file echo feature on or off.

REM (Remark) Command

The **REM** (or remark) command lets you document your batch files, making them more readable. Remarks may display on the screen during execution of the batch file. To direct an inexperienced operator to insert a specific disk during the processing of a batch file, you could include the following command in a batch file:

```
REM INSERT THE DATA DISK INTO DRIVE B AND PRESS ENTER
```

However, the operator does not have time to read the message, much less take the appropriate action, before the next batch file command executes. Fortunately, DOS provides a method for pausing execution long enough to allow the user to do something before continuing.

PAUSE Command

The **PAUSE** command temporarily halts execution of a batch file. It halts execution at the PAUSE command in the batch file and displays the message "Press any key when ready …" on the screen. The next batch file command is processed after the user enters a keystroke.

ECHO Command

The **ECHO** command also improves communication during execution. If you put ECHO OFF in your batch file, DOS will not display (echo) batch file commands during execution after that point. If you put ECHO ON in your batch file, all subsequent commands (including REM commands) display on the screen. To display a message, even if ECHO is off, use the ECHO command with a message. Sample REM, PAUSE, and ECHO batch file commands are shown in Figure 10.2.

Figure 10.2
Sample Batch File (SS.BAT)

```
ECHO    OFF
REM     BATCH FILE NAMED SS.BAT
ECHO    PROCEDURE TO EXECUTE LOTUS 1-2-3
ECHO    PLACE THE LOTUS DATA DISK IN DRIVE A
PAUSE
CD\SS
LOTUS
```

The sample batch file in Figure 10.2 is executed by entering the batch file name (SS) without the extension. When DOS executes the first command in the batch file, it sets the echo mode off. Thus, the REM command is not displayed. The REM command displays only when the file is viewed with the TYPE command. Both of the ECHO messages display and the system pauses, waiting for any key to be pressed before continuing. Then, the last batch file command runs Lotus 1-2-3. Figure 10.3 shows what the screen display looks like when SS.BAT runs.

Figure 10.3

Screen Messages from the Batch File (SS.BAT)

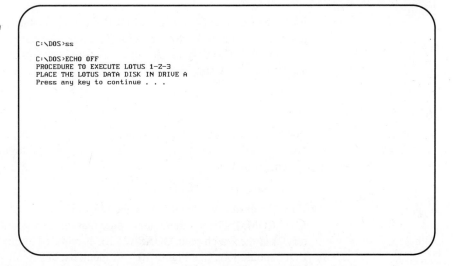

```
C:\DOS>ss

C:\DOS>ECHO OFF
PROCEDURE TO EXECUTE LOTUS 1-2-3
PLACE THE LOTUS DATA DISK IN DRIVE A
Press any key to continue . . .
```

Several additional points about batch files are worth mentioning:

- You can use **@ECHO OFF** to suppress the display of the ECHO OFF command. An @ at the beginning of any batch file line suppresses the display of that line.

- To issue a "beep" in a batch file (for alerting the operator to some action or problem), use **ECHO <Ctrl-G>.**

- You can enter the batch file command **ECHO:** to display a blank line on the screen.

- If you enter **ECHO OFF** at the system prompt, the system prompt disappears until you enter **ECHO ON**, or reboot the system.

- If you press **Ctrl-C** (Ctrl-Break) when a batch file is executing, DOS asks you if you want to terminate the batch job. Respond **Y** to halt the execution of the batch file and return to the system prompt.

- Chapter 14 covers four advanced batch file commands, including IF, CHOICE, FOR, and CALL.

- The COPY CON command is useful for creating small batch files, but it cannot be used to change existing files. Use the EDIT command, discussed next, to create *and* change batch files.

USING THE EDIT COMMAND

Early versions of DOS relied on EDLIN, a cumbersome line-oriented text editor, to create batch files. DOS 6 has a full-screen, menu-based text editing facility called **EDIT**. This easy-to-use editor lets you create text files and change them as often as you wish.

Creating a New Text File

The best way to learn EDIT is to use it! Experiment with it by creating a new text file on Drive A called TESTEDIT.TXT. Enter the following command at the system prompt:

```
A:\> EDIT A:TESTEDIT.TXT
```

If EDIT doesn't run, see if a file called QBASIC.EXE is in the same directory as EDIT.COM. If it is not there, make sure that it can be found in the current directory or in the search path. QBASIC.EXE is required to run EDIT. The screen in EDIT should look like Figure 10.4. A menu bar always displays on the top line. It contains pull-down menus for executing EDIT commands: File, Edit, Search, Options, and Help.

Figure 10.4
Initial EDIT Screen

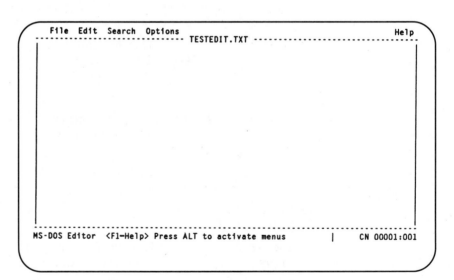

By pressing the Alt key and then the appropriate arrow keys, you can select a variety of tasks from the pull-down menus. Figure 10.5 shows what the File pull-down menu might look like if you were editing a sample text file named PHONE.LST.

Figure 10.5
File Pull-down Menu
in EDIT

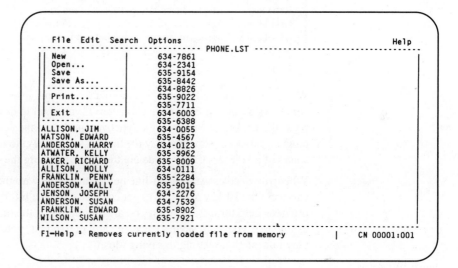

Notice that the bottom right portion of the screen in Figure 10.5 contains 00001:001. These numbers represent the current line number and current cursor position. They can help you enter and change text. Enter the following three lines of text so you can try some of the operations described in the following paragraphs. *Be sure to press the Enter key after each line.*

```
This text file is just for experimenting with EDIT.

It cannot be executed, but it can be displayed on

the screen using the TYPE command.
```

Text is entered in EDIT much like a word processing program with one major exception: each line is limited to 255 characters of text. Because EDIT is most often used with batch files, where each line is relatively short, this limitation is not a problem.

Using a variety of cursor movement keys, you can quickly jump around the screen to insert, change, or delete characters of text. Figure 10.6 identifies eight cursor movement keys.

Figure 10.6
EDIT Cursor
Movement Keys

KEY	FUNCTION
Up arrow	Moves the cursor up one line on the screen.
Down arrow	Moves the cursor down one line on the screen.
Right arrow	Moves the cursor right one character.
Left arrow	Moves the cursor left one character.
Home key	Moves the cursor to the beginning of the line.
END key	Moves the cursor to the end of the line.
Ctrl-Home	Moves the cursor to the top line of the file.
Ctrl-End	Moves the cursor to the bottom line of the file.

When you initially edit a file, you are placed into the insert mode and the cursor shows as an underscore (_) character. If you want to overstrike existing text, press the Ins key to switch to the typeover mode and the cursor shows as a rectangular block. Use the Del key (or the Backspace key) to delete individual characters of text. Press Ctrl-Y to delete the line containing the cursor.

When you need assistance, on-line help is available with the help feature. You can press the F1 key any time to get context-sensitive information. This feature provides help for the operation you are attempting at the time you press F1. For example, if you were saving a text file and pressed F1, your screen would display information relating to saving files.

Using On-line Help

If you need help using EDIT, you can get continual on-line help in the top portion of the screen while working with text in the bottom portion. Whenever you press F1, the screen will be split into two windows, as shown in Figure 10.7.

Figure 10.7
EDIT Help Screen

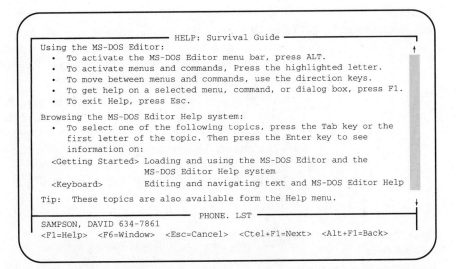

```
                        ┌──────── HELP: Survival Guide ────────┐
 Using the MS-DOS Editor:                                                   ↑
    •  To activate the MS-DOS Editor menu bar, press ALT.
    •  To activate menus and commands, Press the highlighted letter.
    •  To move between menus and commands, use the direction keys.
    •  To get help on a selected menu, command, or dialog box, press F1.
    •  To exit Help, press Esc.
 Browsing the MS-DOS Editor Help system:
    •  To select one of the following topics, press the Tab key or the
       first letter of the topic. Then press the Enter key to see
       information on:
   <Getting Started> Loading and using the MS-DOS Editor and the
                     MS-DOS Editor Help system
   <Keyboard>        Editing and navigating text and MS-DOS Editor Help

 Tip:  These topics are also available form the Help menu.           ↓
                         ── PHONE. LST ──
 SAMPSON, DAVID 634-7861
 <F1=Help>  <F6=Window>  <Esc=Cancel>  <Ctel+F1=Next>  <Alt+F1=Back>
```

The larger window on top displays Help data, while the lower window (initially shown very small) is for entering text. To change the size of the windows, press the Alt key with the plus (or minus) key to increase (or decrease) the size of a window. A list of other commands displays on the bottom line of the EDIT screen. These commands are as follows:

F1   Displays context-sensitive help when you are editing text.

F6   Moves from one window to the other.

Esc   Exits from on-line help and displays text in a single window on the screen.

Ctrl-F1 Browses forward through the Help information. If you have split windows, their size will vary based on the data displayed.

Alt-F1 Browses backward through Help information.

Using the
Pull-down Menus

Many EDIT commands, like the commands to save an edited file or load a new file to be changed, use pull-down menus. Figure 10.8 describes the pull-down menu commands in EDIT. Menus and actions are chosen by typing the **boldface** letter shown, or by clicking on them with a mouse.

The Alt key is used to select items from the Main menu bar. When you are finished entering and changing text, press the Alt key and then the **F** key to display the pull-down menu for File. Because this is the first pull-down menu, you could have also pressed Alt and then the Enter key to do the same thing. Now press the **X** key to exit from EDIT. Enter a response of **N** when asked if you want to save the file. EDIT offers an easy way to create and modify text files.

Figure 10.8
EDIT Pull-down
Menu Commands

MENU	ACTION	DESCRIPTION
File	New	Completely erases everything in memory, letting you create a new text file.
	Open	Displays a dialog box that lets you select a file for editing. Use the Tab key to move to next area within a dialog box.
	Save	Backs up the current text and lets you continue editing.
	Save As	Copies the current text to disk using a filename you specify.
	Print	Sends the current text to the printer.
	EXit	If the current text is not saved, you are prompted to save it before exiting EDIT.
Edit	CuT	Extracts a block of text for later insertion. Hold down Shift key and use arrow keys to mark a block of text.
	Copy	Copies a block of text to another location.
	Paste	Inserts a block of text at the cursor location.
	ClEar	Deletes a block of text.
Search	Find	Locates a specified string of text.
	Repeat Find	Locates another instance of the previous character string used in the last Find action.
	Change	Replaces one string of characters with another.
Options	Display	Lets you change screen colors and display options.
	Help Path	Lets you specify the directory containing the EDIT.HLP file containing on-line Help information.
Help	Getting Started	Displays the initial entry screen to get the set of on-line Help information.
	Keyboard	Displays on-line help related to the keyboard.
	About	Displays the version of EDIT.COM.

Using EDIT from the DOS Shell

The DOS shell includes a *file association* feature that can link all files that share a common extension with a particular program. By default, all TXT files are associated with EDIT. If you double-click on a TXT file in the File List area of the shell, DOS automatically executes the EDIT command for that file. Not only can you view a file with this feature, but you can change the file as well.

Using a Mouse with EDIT

You can use a mouse with EDIT the same way it is used with the DOS shell. Scroll bars are provided for browsing through on-line help information. Pull-down menus are accessed, files are selected, and actions are chosen by clicking on desired items.

Chapter 10

REVIEW QUESTIONS

1. What is the purpose of batch files?
2. How does DOS identify batch files?
3. What are two different ways to create batch files?
4. When is an AUTOEXEC.BAT file executed?
5. What commands would you expect to find in an AUTOEXEC.BAT file?
6. How are variable data (parameters) included in batch files?
7. Why are REM commands used in batch files?
8. When are REM commands in batch files displayed?
9. What is the function of a PAUSE command in a batch file?
10. What happens when you enter ECHO OFF at the system prompt?
11. What will be displayed on the screen when the following batch file commands are executed?

    ```
    @ECHO OFF
    REM SAMPLE BATCH FILE
    ECHO PLACE WP DISK IN DRIVE A
    PAUSE
    ```

12. What does "full-screen text editor" mean?
13. What EDIT command moves the cursor to the bottom line of a file in EDIT?
14. Define a pull-down menu.
15. How are the pull-down menus accessed in EDIT?
16. When using EDIT, what two keys let you delete a character of text?
17. If you are in typeover mode, how do you insert characters of text in EDIT?

18. How can you access on-line help when using EDIT?

19. What File command in EDIT erases the current text in memory?

20. What happens if you attempt to exit EDIT without having first saved the current text you are editing?

Chapter 10

FLOPPY DISK LAB EXERCISES

1. Use EDIT to create a text file.

To begin this exercise, boot DOS, place your data disk in Drive B, and enter **EDIT B:LINEDIT.DOC**. Now you are ready to create a new text file. The text to enter is shown in **boldface** below. Clarification comments are noted in parentheses.

ONE (this is the first line of text)

TWO

THREE

FOUR

FIVE

SIX

SEVEN

EIGHT

NINE

TEN

(use the Up arrow key to move the cursor to the "F" in FOUR)

(press the Del key five times to entirely delete that line of text)

(use the Down arrow key to position the cursor at the beginning of the line of text after TEN)

ELEVEN (this is the next line of text to be added)

TWELVE (this is the last line of text to be added)

(use the Up arrow key to move to the line of text containing THREE)

(press the End key to move to the end of that line)

(press the Enter key to insert a blank line of text)

FOUR (the Enter key is not required here)

(press the Alt key to access the menu line)

(press the Down arrow key to view the pull-down menu)

(press S to save the file to disk with the filename previously given)

(press the Alt key and Down arrow key again to view the File menu)

(press X to exit the EDIT command)

2. Practice using EDIT by entering **EDIT B:LINEDIT.DOC** to recall the previous text file.

   Delete the last two lines in the file, ELEVEN and TWELVE. Immediately after the line containing FIVE, insert a line containing ELEVEN. Then add two lines at the bottom of the file for TWELVE and THIRTEEN. Except for one line, the file of text should be in numeric sequence. See how long it takes to edit the file to make it all in sequence by numerical value. Save this file when you exit EDIT. What would happen if, after leaving EDIT, you sorted this file using the SORT command without the /R option?

3. Set up a batch file (**FORMAT.BAT**) to prevent anyone from formatting a disk on Drive A by mistake. This batch file will only permit FORMAT to format a disk on Drive B. Enter:

   REN FORMAT.COM FORMATB.COM (renames the FORMAT command)

   COPY CON FORMAT.BAT (quickly creates a one-line batch file)

   FORMATB B:<F6>

   Notice that the original FORMAT command was renamed so you could use FORMAT as the new batch file name. Then the batch file is used to execute the renamed format command (FORMATB) with the desired option, the formatting of Drive B only.

   Remove the disk in Drive B and enter **FORMAT** to execute the batch file just created. When you get the message to insert a blank disk in Drive B, press Ctrl-Break (or Ctrl-C) to stop further execution of this command. Figure 10.9 shows what the screen should look like after you execute FORMAT.BAT.

Figure 10.9
**Screen Display after
Executing FORMAT.BAT**

```
C:\DOS>copy con format.bat
formatb b:^Z
        1 file(s) copied

C:\DOS>format

C:\DOS>formatb b:
Insert new diskette for drive B:
and press ENTER when ready...^C


C:\DOS>
```

Note: Before you continue to the next step, delete FORMAT.BAT and then rename FORMATB.COM to FORMAT.COM. Can you think of any other commands you would like to create?

4. Use **EDIT B:AUTOEXEC.BAT** to create a batch file on your data disk containing the following commands:

```
@ECHO OFF
REM SAMPLE INITIALIZATION PROCEDURE
DATE
TIME
ECHO ON
PAUSE PLACE DATA DISK IN DRIVE B
DIR A: > B:DISKA.DIR
DIR B:
REM END OF INITIALIZATION
ECHO OFF
ECHO HAVE A NICE DAY
PROMPT DATE IS $D $_TIME IS $T $_WHAT NEXT?
```

When you are done, execute this new batch file. Experiment with entering a few commands such as TIME, VER, and VOL with the new prompt. Then enter **PROMPT PG** to change the system prompt to display the current directory.

5. Use EDIT to build a simple batch file (**OFF.BAT**) that clears the screen when executed. Include the following three commands in this screen saver:

```
@ECHO OFF

CLS

PAUSE >NUL
```

The output of the PAUSE command, "Press any key to continue …", is redirected to the NUL device so it will not display on the screen. After executing this command, press any key to return to the system prompt and continue working.

6. Use COPY CON to create a short batch file (**TOP.BAT**) that will advance most Epson- or IBM-compatible printers to the top of the page. These printers recognize Ctrl-L as a form-feed character. If you are connected to an appropriate printer, you can test this batch file. The batch file contains three commands as follows:

```
REM TOP.BAT TO ADVANCE PAGE TO THE TOP OF FORM

ECHO OFF

ECHO <Ctrl-L> >PRN
```

When typing the last line, press the spacebar after ECHO, then press Ctrl-L followed by another space before typing >PRN.

7. For additional work, build a batch file on your data disk with EDIT to create a new command for you. This batch file (**MOV.BAT**) lets you copy a file, give it another name, and then delete the original name. The new batch file should contain the following:

```
COPY %1 %2

DEL %1
```

This new batch file is executed by entering the batch file name (B:MOV) followed by two parameters (for %1 and %2). The parameter %1 represents the original filename and %2 represents the new filename. Enter **B:MOV B:TEST3.DIR B:TEST5.DIR**.

B:TEST3.DIR is now renamed B:TEST5.DIR. You could have specified that the new file was to be created on Drive A instead of Drive B.

This completes the Chapter 10 floppy disk lab exercises. Remove your disk(s) before you leave the computer.

Chapter 10

HARD DISK LAB EXERCISES

1. Use EDIT to create a text file.

   To begin this exercise, boot DOS, place your data disk in Drive A, and enter **EDIT A:LINEDIT.DOC**. Now you are ready to create a new text file. The text to enter is shown in Exercise 1 of the floppy disk lab exercises, above. Clarification comments are noted in parentheses.

2. Practice using EDIT by entering **EDIT A:LINEDIT.DOC** to recall the previous text file.

   Delete the last two lines in the file, ELEVEN and TWELVE. Immediately after the line containing FIVE, insert a line containing ELEVEN. Then add two lines at the bottom of the file for TWELVE and THIRTEEN. Except for one line, the file of text should be in numeric sequence. See how long it takes to edit the file to make it all in sequence by numerical value. Save this file when you exit EDIT. What would happen if, after leaving EDIT, you sorted this file using the SORT command without the /R option?

3. Set up a batch file (**FORMAT.BAT**) to prevent anyone from formatting a disk on Drive C by mistake. This batch file will only permit FORMAT to format a disk on Drive A. Enter:

   REN FORMAT.COM FORMATA.COM (renames the FORMAT command)

   COPY CON FORMAT.BAT (quickly creates a one-line batch file)

   FORMATA A:<F6>

   Notice that the original FORMAT command was renamed so you could use FORMAT as the new batch file name. Then the batch file is used to execute the renamed format command (FORMATA) with the desired option, the formatting of Drive A only.

   Remove the disk in Drive A and enter **FORMAT** to execute the batch file just created. When you get the message to insert a blank disk in Drive A, press Ctrl-Break (or Ctrl-C) to stop further execution of this command. Figure 10.9 shows what the screen should look like after you execute FORMAT.BAT.

   Note: Before you continue to the next step, delete FORMAT.BAT and then rename FORMATA.COM to FORMAT.COM. Can you think of any other commands you would like to create?

4. Use **EDIT A:AUTOEXEC.BAT** to create a batch file on your data disk containing the following commands:

```
@ECHO OFF
REM SAMPLE INITIALIZATION PROCEDURE
DATE
```

```
TIME
ECHO ON
PAUSE PLACE DATA DISK IN DRIVE A
DIR C: > A:DISKC.DIR
DIR A:
REM END OF INITIALIZATION
ECHO OFF
ECHO HAVE A NICE DAY
PROMPT DATE IS $D $_TIME IS $T $_WHAT NEXT?
```

When you are done, execute this new batch file. Experiment with entering a few commands such as TIME, VER, and VOL with the new prompt. Then enter **PROMPT PG** to change the system prompt to display the current directory.

5. Use EDIT to build a simple batch file (**OFF.BAT**) that clears the screen when executed. Include the following three commands in this screen saver:

```
@ECHO OFF
CLS
PAUSE >NUL
```

The output of the PAUSE command, "Press any key to continue ..", is redirected to the NUL device so it will not display on the screen. After executing this command, press any key to return to the system prompt and continue working.

6. Use COPY CON to create a short batch file (**TOP.BAT**) that will advance most Epson- or IBM-compatible printers to the top of the page. These printers recognize Ctrl-L as a form-feed character. If you are connected to an appropriate printer, you can test this batch file. The batch file contains three commands as follows:

```
REM TOP.BAT TO ADVANCE PAGE TO THE TOP OF FORM
ECHO OFF
ECHO <Ctrl-L> >PRN
```

When typing the last line, press the spacebar after ECHO, then press Ctrl-L followed by another space before typing >PRN.

7. For additional work, build a batch file on your data disk with EDIT to create a new command for you. This batch file (**MOV.BAT**) lets you copy a file, give it another name, and then delete the original name. The new batch file should contain the following:

```
COPY %1 %2

DEL %1
```

This new batch file is be executed by entering the batch file name (A:MOV) followed by two parameters (for %1 and %2). The parameter %1 represents the original filename and %2 represents the new filename. Enter **A:MOV A:TEST3.DIR A:TEST5.DIR**.

A:TEST3.DIR is now renamed A:TEST5.DIR. You could have specified that the new file was to be created on Drive C instead of Drive A.

This completes the Chapter 10 hard disk lab exercises. Remove your data disk before you leave the computer.

CUSTOMIZING DOS

CONFIG.SYS FILE

ANSI.SYS FILE

RAMDRIVE.SYS FILE

SELECTIVE BOOTING

MULTIPLE CONFIGURATIONS

CUSTOMIZING DOS

When DOS was first introduced (1981), the amount of RAM was severely limited compared with today's PCs. It was not uncommon to have a PC with only 256KB of RAM. DOS is designed to work with these smaller systems, but the default settings are not the most efficient for today's larger-RAM machines. Fortunately, DOS lets you reconfigure your system to take advantage of additional RAM.

DOS provides several ways to customize your system. Even if your system was customized by someone else, you can use what you learn in this chapter to revise the configuration. We begin with the CONFIG.SYS file, which automatically configures your system according to your specifications during the boot process. Later we discuss how to use CONFIG.SYS to load instructions into additional memory, freeing up space in regular memory for processing applications.

CONFIG.SYS FILE

CONFIG.SYS is a special file of commands that lets you specify how your system should operate and be configured. It lets you control the way memory is used and install driver programs that control I/O devices.

During the boot process, DOS looks for a CONFIG.SYS file on the root directory of the disk used to boot DOS. If found, all valid commands in the CONFIG.SYS file are executed by DOS. If the CONFIG.SYS file is not found, the system is initialized according to the DOS default values. Avoid booting with these default values, as they are too restricting. CONFIG.SYS is similar to a batch file in that it is a text file of commands, usually created with the EDIT command. Here are the configuration commands that you will most likely use:

BREAK=ON tells DOS that you want it to also check for a Ctrl-C (or Ctrl-Break) entry from the keyboard during disk operations. By default, DOS only checks for a Ctrl-Break during keyboard or screen operations. Thus, if no screen or keyboard operations are being executed, pressing the Ctrl-Break key is ignored by DOS unless BREAK is set ON.

BUFFERS=nn, where nn is the number of input/output buffers needed to improve disk performance. By specifying a higher number of buffers, you tell DOS to read a larger chunk of data from your disk into RAM every time. Data stored in RAM is instantly available. The next time your program needs data, DOS checks to see if it is already in the RAM buffer. A recommended setting of 20 buffers will suit most circumstances. Each buffer uses 512 bytes of memory. It may require some experimenting to find the most effective buffer size for your system, especially if you are running sophisticated applications.

FILES=nn, where nn is the number of files that can be used at once by your programs. The DOS default is only eight. It is recommended that you have at least 40 files specified, as the number of open files include the hidden system files, COMMAND.COM, and Terminate-and-Stay-Resident (TSR) programs. Database and Windows applications often require 30 to 40 files open at a time.

SHELL=xxx, where xxx represents the name of the command interpreter to load. The default command interpreter is the COMMAND.COM file. Although the SHELL command can be used to specify a different command interpreter, SHELL is most often used to increase the size of your environment space. The DOS environment is space allocated to keep track of the values you assign to PATH, PROMPT, and DIRCMD variables. It also keeps track of other arbitrarily named variables used by application programs. As you install more programs that use the environment, such as Windows, you may run out of environment space. If you use the MEMMAKER command (see Chapter 13) to optimize your system memory, you should increase the environment space to 1024 bytes. The SHELL command in Figure 11.1 increases the environment size from its default of 256 bytes to 1024 bytes. The maximum size is 32KB.

DEVICE=xxx, where xxx represents a particular device driver, such as ANSI.SYS, MOUSE.SYS, or RAMDRIVE.SYS. Some device drivers are short programs that tell DOS how to handle input/output from a given device, such as a keyboard, disk, or mouse. A configuration command must be supplied for each device you wish to install.

Figure 11.1 shows sample commands often included in a CONFIG.SYS file. Additional commands related to memory management are covered in Chapter 13. The DOS Help system's Main menu screen includes a topic called "CONFIG.SYS commands." Use it whenever you want more specific information on using the CONFIG.SYS file.

Figure 11.1
Sample CONFIG.SYS File

```
REM SAMPLE CONFIG.SYS FILE
BREAK=ON
FILES=40
BUFFERS=20
SHELL=COMMAND.COM /E:1024 /P
DEVICE=C:\DOS\ANSI.SYS.
DEVICE=C:\DOS\RAMDRIVE.SYS 128
```

ANSI.SYS FILE

ANSI.SYS is a device driver that acts as an interface between the monitor and DOS, and between the keyboard and DOS. It changes the colors on the screen, the number of lines on the screen, or redefines the function keys on the keyboard. The American National Standards Institute (ANSI) has a special set of codes used to control the keyboard and monitor. These codes are activated by a special "escape sequence" of control codes, which can be used only when ANSI.SYS is installed. To install ANSI.SYS, include it as a device driver in the CONFIG.SYS file. If the ANSI.SYS file resides in your DOS subdirectory, use the full filename as shown in Figure 11.1.

ANSI.SYS can also change the way characters display on the screen, including the colors. By using the PROMPT command to send DOS an appropriate escape sequence, you can change screen attributes by using the color codes listed in Figure 11.2.

Figure 11.2
ANSI Color and Attribute Codes

CODE	ATTRIBUTE SETTING	CODE	ATTRIBUTE SETTING
0	All attributes off	35	Foreground magenta
1	High intensity on	36	Foreground cyan
4	Underscored (monochrome only)	37	Foreground white
5	Blinking on	40	Background black
7	Inverse (dark on light)	41	Background red
8	Invisible display	42	Background green
30	Foreground black	43	Background yellow
31	Foreground red	44	Background blue
32	Foreground green	45	Background magenta
33	Foreground yellow	46	Background cyan
34	Foreground blue	47	Background white

The syntax of the PROMPT command used to change the attributes of the screen is complex. The character string **$E[** is required to send an escape sequence to ANSI.SYS. A semicolon separates the screen attributes and a lowercase "m" ends the attribute specifications. In addition, when you use the PROMPT command, you should include the desired system prompt, such as PG, at the end of the command. Use the CLS command after a change of colors to clear the screen to the new colors.

Examples of usage:

```
C:\DOS> PROMPT $E[7m$P$G
```
(sets the monitor to display inverse characters; dark text on a light background)

```
C:\DOS> PROMPT $E[0m$P$G
```
(resets the screen attributes back to normal)

```
C:\DOS> PROMPT $E[37;44m$P$G
```
(displays white foreground characters on a blue background)

```
C:\DOS> PROMPT $E[5m$P$G$E[0m
```
(causes the system prompt to blink and then returns to the normal mode for other text)

```
C:\DOS> PROMPT $E[1mWhat Next?$E[0m
```
(turns high intensity on for the system prompt "What Next?" and then turns it off for other characters)

RAMDRIVE.SYS FILE

RAMDRIVE.SYS (VDISK.SYS in PC-DOS) is a RAM-resident device driver that lets you allocate part of main memory as a simulated disk. It is often called a RAM disk. Access speeds in RAM are much faster than those of a hard disk, so files loaded into a RAM disk are accessed almost immediately. DOS always creates the RAM disk drive designator using the next available disk drive letter, normally as Drive D.

To install the RAM disk capability, you must have RAMDRIVE.SYS included as a device driver in your CONFIG.SYS file. You should specify more than the default of 64KB of RAM allocated to the RAM disk. If your RAMDRIVE.SYS file resides in your DOS subdirectory, include the CONFIG.SYS entry as shown in Figure 11.1 to establish a 128KB RAM disk. If you have additional RAM (2–8MB), you can create a much larger RAM disk in extended memory. This subject is explained further in Chapter 13.

As part of your AUTOEXEC.BAT file, you should copy any external DOS commands, batch files, and programs that you expect to execute most often into the RAM disk area. In addition, your PATH command should include the new RAM disk drive. For example:

```
COPY C:\WP\WORD.* D:
PATH = D:\;C:\DOS;C:\UTIL
```

Now you can execute your word processing program from Drive D instead of Drive C. It will execute much faster from the RAM disk than from your hard disk. Only program files should be loaded to a RAM disk, however. It is a dangerous practice to put data files on a RAM disk, because valuable data could be lost during power failures or surges. If you do have any data files on RAM disk, be sure to save them to permanent disk storage with the COPY or XCOPY command before turning off the CPU.

SELECTIVE BOOTING

There may be times when you boot your system that it will get "hung up" trying to execute a command in the CONFIG.SYS file. DOS 6 provides a method of performing a selective boot. **Selective booting** lets you decide which lines in the CONFIG.SYS file execute. In addition, you can direct DOS to bypass executing your AUTOEXEC.BAT file.

To do a selective boot, press the F8 function key as soon as the "Starting MS-DOS..." displays during the boot process. By default, DOS waits two seconds after displaying this message before proceeding with the boot. During the selective boot, DOS prompts you to confirm execution of each CONFIG.SYS command. Beginning with Version 6.2 of DOS, the F8 key also prompts you to confirm each command in your AUTOEXEC.BAT file.

The selective boot provides an excellent way to examine each startup command and determine which one is causing you problems. Once you locate the problem, boot the system bypassing the problem command. Then, use EDIT to correct the CONFIG.SYS and/or AUTOEXEC.BAT file and reboot without using the F8 key to test your changes.

If passwords are required to complete the boot process, then anyone can use the F8 key to selectively skip over problem commands in the CONFIG.SYS and AUTOEXEC.BAT files. To remove the selective booting feature of DOS, add **SWITCHES = / N** as the first command of your CONFIG.SYS file.

MULTIPLE CONFIGURATIONS

At startup, the multiconfiguration feature of DOS 6 lets you choose a boot configuration from a customized menu. This is very useful if you have several different ways to configure your system, such as with or without using Windows, or with or without connecting to a Local Area Network. Using a menu, it lets you select what commands in the CONFIG.SYS and AUTOEXEC.BAT files execute during startup.

To use this feature, each section of the CONFIG.SYS file must be labeled with a name enclosed in brackets. Figure 11.3 shows a sample structure of a CONFIG.SYS file for multiple configurations. All it is missing are the specific CONFIG.SYS commands used for each type of configuration. You can use this example to create your own menu-driven startup. The first two section names shown below (menu and common) are reserved for special sections.

Figure 11.3
**Sample CONFIG.SYS File
with Menu Selections**

```
[menu]
menuitem=WIN, Windows
menuitem=DOS,DOS 6.2
menuitem=LAN, Local Area Network
menudefault=LAN,10
menucolor=15,1
[common]
```
(commands common to all menu selections)
```
[WIN]
```
(additional commands used for Windows)
```
SET CONFIG=WIN
[DOS]
```
(commands used when Windows will not be used)
```
SET CONFIG=DOS
[LAN]
```
(commands used to connect to the LAN)
```
SET CONFIG=LAN
```

The [menu] section defines the startup menu. Menu items display on the screen, giving the user a choice of startup commands to execute. The commands listed in the [common] section apply to all configurations. In this example, the system is directed to default to the LAN section if a menu selection is not made within ten seconds. The menu colors can also be customized. Here, the menu colors are bright white foreground on a blue background. Use **HELP MENUCOLOR** to view the color codes.

The **SET command** at the end of each menu item section tells DOS which section of the AUTOEXEC.BAT file to execute. Figure 11.4 shows a sample structure of an AUTOEXEC.BAT file used with the previous CONFIG.SYS file. Although it is not complete, it can easily be used as a beginning point to customize your own startup.

Figure 11.4

Sample AUTOEXEC.BAT File for Multiple Configurations

```
@ECHO OFF
(commands common to all sections)
GOTO %CONFIG%
:WIN
(commands to boot DOS and load Windows)
.GOTO END
:DOS
(commands to boot to DOS only)
.GOTO END
:LAN
(commands to connect to the LAN)
:END
```

In this sample AUTOEXEC.BAT file, the first two commands are common to all sections. Sections must be identified with a colon preceding the section name, such as :WIN. Likewise, the end of the batch file is identified with the name :END. The batch file command GOTO is used to skip past unwanted sections. Here, the first GOTO branches to the section named in the CONFIG environment variable, which was set in the CONFIG.SYS file. When the desired section is finished, the GOTO command is also used to skip to the end of the batch file (if required).

With the multiconfiguration feature, you no longer need to continually switch and rename different versions of your CONFIG.SYS and AUTOEXEC.BAT files. Nor do you need to press the F8 key to control how DOS boots. It takes a little time to create the menus, but it is time well spent.

Chapter 11

REVIEW QUESTIONS

1. Why would you want to customize the way DOS runs?

2. What do you think it means when someone says "DOS is downward (backward) compatible?"

3. What is the purpose of the CONFIG.SYS file?

4. How is a CONFIG.SYS file typically created?

5. What is the importance of increasing the number of default values for buffers and open files in DOS?

6. What file is the default command interpreter for DOS?

7. What is the DOS environment?

8. How do you increase the size of the DOS environment?

9. What is a device driver?

10. What is the purpose of the ANSI.SYS file?

11. Why is the PROMPT command often required to modify screen colors?

12. Specifically, what PROMPT command is entered to display black text on a yellow background?

13. What must occur before you can execute a PROMPT command to change screen colors?

14. What device driver is used to create a RAM disk?

15. Why might it be dangerous to load data files to a RAM disk?

16. What command is used to load a mouse driver in DOS?

17. Why would you want to boot your system using multiple configurations?

18. Under what circumstances would you include BREAK=ON in your CONFIG.SYS file?

19. What color code (or codes) allow a password typed without showing on the screen?

20. How does selective booting let you locate a problem in your CONFIG.SYS file?

Chapter 11

FLOPPY DISK LAB EXERCISES

1. Assume you will be leaving your computer for a short time and want to discourage novice users from using your system. By entering ECHO OFF followed by CLS, your screen will become blank with just the flashing cursor. Experiment with this by running some commands without any prompt displayed. Then restore the prompt by turning ECHO back ON.

2. Use EDIT to create a CONFIG.SYS file on Drive A that will provide for up to 35 open files and 20 buffers in DOS, and install ANSI.SYS. If you have a color monitor, experiment with changing the colors of the screen. Don't forget to reboot your system to activate the ANSI.SYS file.

3. Create a batch file (**COLORS.BAT**) that will let you experiment with the screen colors once ANSI.SYS is installed as a device driver in the CONFIG.SYS file. This batch file is as follows:

```
REM COLORS.BAT TO TEST SCREEN COLORS
PROMPT $E[%1;%2m$P$G
CLS
DIR /W
```

Install ANSI.SYS and execute COLORS.BAT several times, including the following three examples:

```
COLORS 33 40
COLORS 37 44
COLORS 30 46
```

This completes the Chapter 11 floppy disk lab exercises. Remove your disk(s) before you leave the computer.

Chapter 11

HARD DISK LAB EXERCISES

1. Assume you will be leaving your computer for a short time and want to discourage novice users from using your system. By entering ECHO OFF followed by CLS, your screen will become blank with just the flashing cursor. Experiment with this by running some commands without any prompt displayed. Then restore the prompt by turning echo back ON.

2. Use EDIT to create a CONFIG.SYS file on Drive A that will provide for up to 35 open files and 20 buffers in DOS, and install ANSI.SYS.

3. Assume for the moment that you have a system with a hard disk and only one floppy disk. You want to make a backup copy of a floppy disk that contains data not on your hard disk. Create and test a batch file called C:\DOS\BKUP.BAT that simplifies this process, one you anticipate performing often. The batch file should contain the following statements:

```
REM BACKUP A FLOPPY DISK ONTO ANOTHER FLOPPY USING
REM A ONE-FLOPPY, SINGLE HARD DISK SYSTEM.
REM
MD C:\TEMP8765
REM INSERT ORIGINAL FLOPPY IN DRIVE A:
PAUSE
COPY A:*.* C:\TEMP8765
REM INSERT BLANK FLOPPY IN DRIVE A:
PAUSE
FORMAT A: (or FORMAT A:/F:720, if 720KB disk in 1.44MB Drive)
COPY C:\TEMP8765\*.* A:
REM
REM RESPOND WITH "Y" TO THE ARE YOU SURE? PROMPT
REM
DEL C:\TEMP8765\*.*
```

```
RD C:\TEMP8765
REM END OF BACKUP
DIR A:/P
```

4. Create a batch file (**COLORS.BAT**) that will let you experiment with the screen colors once ANSI.SYS is installed as a device driver in the CONFIG.SYS file. This batch file is as follows:

```
REM COLORS.BAT TO TEST SCREEN COLORS
PROMPT $E[%1;%2m$P$G
CLS
DIR /W
```

Install ANSI.SYS and execute COLORS.BAT several times, including the following three examples:

```
COLORS 33 40
COLORS 37 44
COLORS 30 46
```

This completes the Chapter 11 hard disk lab exercises. Remove your data disk before you leave the computer.

ADVANCED DOS COMMANDS

DBLSPACE (Disk Compression) Command

FDISK (Partition Disk) Command

MODE Command

MSD (Display System Information) Command

PRINT Command

SET Command

SETVER (Set Version) Command

SMARTDRV (Disk Caching) Command

SYS (System) Command

Each DOS command covered in this chapter may be required from time to time. The objective is to acquaint you with these commands so you can use them if the need arises. The following advanced commands are covered:

DBLSPACE	Automatically compresses data, effectively doubling the amount of data that can be stored on a disk.
FDISK	Configures a hard disk for use with MS-DOS.
MODE	Modifies system parameters for input/output devices.
MSD	Provides detailed technical information about your system.
PRINT	Allows text files to print while DOS executes other commands.
SET	Sets the DOS environment variables.
SETVER	Lets you control the DOS version reported to a specific program, if an older version of DOS is required.
SMARTDRV	Lets your system perform disk caching to improve disk access.
SYS	Creates a bootable DOS disk.

DBLSPACE (Disk Compression) Command (external)

Syntax: `DBLSPACE`

One of the most controversial features of DOS 6 is the DoubleSpace utility program, which can nearly double the number of bytes you can store on a disk. **DBLSPACE** is the MS-DOS version of this disk compression program. To compress a hard disk, DBLSPACE redefines the disk into two parts:

1. In the first part, DBLSPACE stores all the files it compresses into one huge file called CVF (Compressed Volume File). If you used to see Drive C as 40MB of total space, it will now show nearly 80MB of space. Except for this increase in size, you will not likely see any difference in the way files are processed on disk.

2. The second part contains all the files that must remain uncompressed, like hidden system files. Normally labeled Drive H, it generally goes unnoticed by the user.

So how do files get compressed? Although you don't need to know how DBLSPACE compresses files to take advantage of the feature, a brief explanation is offered here to satisfy the curious.

Most files contain lots of repeated data. When DBLSPACE finds repeated data in a file, it retains just the first occurrence of that data. It replaces subsequent occurrences of that data with a cross-reference to the first occurrence. A cross-referencing symbol takes less space than the original data.

For example, suppose a text file contained the phrase "they left the theater by the side door." DBLSPACE substitutes the repeated instances of " the" with the @ character. This phrase is stored as " they left@@ater by@ side door", using 25% fewer bytes. Database and spreadsheet files contain many repeated characters, including large groups of spaces. They typically have a higher compression ratio than do text files.

DBLSPACE must be run initially to compress all files on a disk. Then, it must be loaded in RAM each time you boot DOS. The first time you run DBLSPACE, you will see a welcome message similar to Figure 12.1.

Figure 12.1
DBLSPACE Welcome Message

```
Welcome to DoubleSpace Setup
The Setup program for DoubleSpace frees space on your hard
disk by compressing the existing files on the disk. Setup
also loads DBLSPACE.BIN, the portion of MS-DOS that provides
access to DoubleSpace compressed drives. DBLSPACE.BIN
requires about 40K of memory.
If you use a network, then before installing DoubleSpace,
start the network and connect to any drives you normally use.
    • To set up DoubleSpace now, press ENTER.
    • To learn more about DoubleSpace Setup, press F1.
    • To quit Setup without installing DoubleSpace, press F3.
```

When you press the Enter key to set up DBLSPACE, you are asked if you want to run the Express Setup or the Custom Setup. Unless you know what you are doing, *the Express Setup is recommended.* After the disk is checked for errors, the data to be compressed is examined and the estimated amount of time it will take is displayed. A 40MB hard disk will take roughly 30 minutes to compress. Once compression is finished, DBLSPACE executes the DEFRAG command to reorganize the files for optimal access. Then, DBLSPACE displays the following information:

• How much space you had before and after compression.

• The ratio at which DBLSPACE compressed your files.

• The amount of time it took to compress the disk.

As the final step in this process, DBLSPACE automatically updates your CONFIG.SYS and AUTOEXEC.BAT files for you. These changes are required to tell DOS your disk is compressed and to load DBLSPACE.BIN each time you boot. Now you can work with compressed files just like you did before compression with one exception: it may take 10-15% longer to read and write files once they are compressed.

Here are some additional points to consider:

- Although you can compress floppy disks, you probably don't want to as they can only be used on a computer with DBLSPACE loaded.

- Defragmentation of a compressed disk takes much longer than it does on disks that have not been compressed.

- Before you make significant changes to your system, you should protect yourself by making backup copies of important files.

- You should begin using compressed disks only if space on your hard drive becomes scarce. If you run CHKDSK and it shows you have less than 5MB, or you have a large software package to load, it's time to compress.

- In DOS 6.0 you could not decompress your hard disk once you used DBLSPACE. Version 6.2 added an option to remove DBLSPACE.

- Because the DBLSPACE device driver, DBLSPACE.BIN, requires at least 40MB of RAM, it should be loaded in upper memory. This is done by adding the following command (covered in the next chapter) to your CONFIG.SYS file:

```
DEVICEHIGH=C:\DOS\DBLSPACE.SYS /MOVE
```

FDISK (Partition Disk) Command (external)

Syntax: FDISK /STATUS

The **FDISK** command creates and manages partitions on a hard disk. Thus, it normally loads from a DOS disk in Drive A. Even if you want just one partition, you must still run FDISK to configure your hard disk to use DOS. Normally, you will only have a single hard disk partition, devoted exclusively to DOS. However, a second partition could be reserved for another operating system, such as UNIX. FDISK lets you create a partition, adjust the size of a partition, change from one partition to another, or delete a partition.

The **/STATUS** option displays an overview of the partition information of your hard disk only. It can be used to quickly view partition information without executing the partitioning process.

Each partition becomes a logical disk drive, where one drive is the boot drive. For example, you can partition your hard disk into two logical disks, Drive C and Drive D. Drive C is the DOS boot disk containing all your programs and Drive D stores all your data files. Having all data files on one drive simplifies the backup process.

When you install a new hard disk, execute FDISK and chose Option 1, "Create Primary DOS partition." The system then asks if you want to use the entire hard disk system for DOS. If you do, respond with **Y**. Otherwise, respond with **N** and consult the DOS on-line help facility for further instructions. **Warning:** Do not experiment with FDISK. When you create a partition on an established hard disk, all data on the disk is erased.

After the hard disk partition is created, you must run FORMAT with the /S option to make it bootable with DOS. Then you should copy COMMAND.COM and all the DOS external commands to a directory (e.g., \DOS) and store your DOS floppy disk for safekeeping. Once this process is completed, you can boot the system from the hard disk.

Examples of usage:

A:\> FDISK
(loads the FDISK program so you can create or modify partitions on your hard disk)

C:\DOS> FDISK /STATUS
(displays partition information about your computer's hard disk)

MODE Command (external)

The **MODE** command sets the operational modes of the printer, monitor, keyboard, and communication ports. It lets you reconfigure the way those system devices operate. Consequently, there are many different forms of the MODE command. Three forms you might use are discussed below. Refer to a DOS manual for additional information.

Syntax for the Printer: [d:]MODE LPTx cpl,lpi

This form of the MODE command lets you specify how characters are printed for any printer that is IBM- or Epson-compatible. Thus, you can print 132 characters on a print line instead of the usual 80. The character x is the printer number (1–3), *cpl* is the characters per line (80 or 132), and *lpi* is the number of lines per vertical inch (6 or 8). When executed, MODE sends the appropriate control codes to the printer. The default settings are 80 characters per line and 6 lines per inch.

Examples of usage:

C:\DOS> MODE LPT1 132,8
(sets the printer connected to LPT1 to compressed print at 8 lines per inch)

C:\DOS> mode lpt1 132
(sets the LPT1 printer to compressed print using the default of 6 lines per inch)

C:\DOS> MODE LPT1 COM1
(changes from parallel printer port LPT1 to a serial COM port)

Syntax for the Keyboard: [d:]MODE CON RATE=x DELAY=y

This form of the MODE command lets you change the speed of the keyboard on newer systems. The result is faster processing, especially if you like to use your arrow keys to move around the screen or scroll the display screen. The rate at which the cursor moves can be from 1 to 32. The default rate is 20 on most keyboards. If you set the rate, you must also set the delay. The delay specifies the amount of time before the repeating key feature begins when you hold down a key. Valid values for the delay are from 1 to 4, representing 1/4, 1/2, 3/4, and 1 second, respectively. The default is 2 (1/2 second).

Examples of usage:

C:\DOS> MODE CON RATE=1 DELAY=4
(sets the speed of the keyboard to be extremely slow)

C:\DOS> mode con rate=32 delay=1
(sets the speed of the keyboard to be extremely fast)

C:\DOS> mode con rate=20 delay=2
(returns the keyboard speeds to the original default speeds)

Syntax for the Monitor: [d:]MODE CON [COLS=c] [LINES=n]

This form of MODE sets the number of lines displayed on a VGA screen or the number of columns displayed on any screen. The valid value for the number of columns is 40 or 80. If you have trouble viewing characters on the screen, you can make characters twice as large with a setting of 40. The valid values for the number of lines are 25, 43, or 50. With this command you can have DOS display 43 or 50 lines instead of the usual 25. Length-sensitive DOS commands like CLS and MORE recognize the new screen sizes and adjust themselves accordingly. When using MODE to set the number of lines, the ANSI.SYS device driver must be installed via the CONFIG.SYS file.

Examples of usage:

C:\DOS> mode con cols=40
(sets the screen to display 40 characters per line)

C:\DOS> mode con lines=43
(sets a VGA monitor to display 43 lines)

C:\DOS> MODE CON LINES=25
(resets the monitor to the default of 25 lines)

**MSD (Display System
Information) Command
(external)**

Syntax: `[d:][path]MSD [/P filename]`

The **MSD** command displays technical information about your computer. It has
been available to Windows 3.1 users for several years. MSD was used as a tool
to help Microsoft diagnose problems when people called them for help. This
command can help to identify interrupt (IRQ) problems on your system. Figure
12.2 shows a sample MSD screen used to find information about different hardware components of a system.

Figure 12.2

Sample MSD Screen

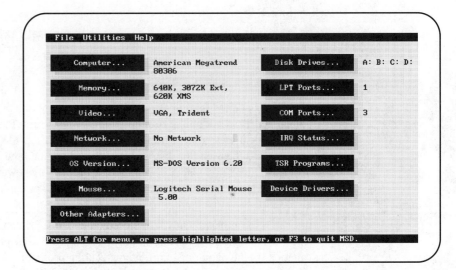

You can use your mouse (or the cursor movement keys) to obtain further information on each of these 13 hardware categories displayed on the MSD screen. It
includes information relating to the type of ROM chip used, the allocation of
memory from 640KB to 1024KB, the mouse interrupt request line (IRQ) number, the location and size of TSR programs loaded, and the names of device drivers installed. Refer to the DOS manual (or use the on-line help facility) to see
additional information reported for each category.

The **/P** option creates a file containing a detailed report about your computer.
You must provide a filename with this option. This text file can be viewed with
the EDIT command or printed with the COPY command.

Examples of usage:

C:\DOS> MSD

(displays categories of hardware information about your system and lets you examine each category in greater detail)

C:\DOS> MSD /P A:HARDWARE.TXT

(creates a file on Drive A called HARDWARE.TXT containing detailed hardware information about your system)

PRINT Command
(external, TSR)

Syntax: [d:][path]PRINT [/D:device] [/B:size] [/S:time]

or

[d:][path]PRINT [d:][path]filename[.ext] [/P] [/C]

or

[d:][path]PRINT [/T]

The printer operates extremely slowly compared with the processing speed of computers. Thus, a small portion of computer resources (RAM space and clock time) can be allocated to printing (executing PRINT), while the majority of resources can be used for other processing at the same time. When you use the TYPE or COPY commands to print a disk file, you must wait until all printing is completed before executing another DOS command or application program.

You can avoid lengthy delays when you have long documents to print by using the **PRINT** command. Only files stored on disk in a printable format (ASCII text files) may be added to a print queue (list of files to be printed). Thus, PRINT cannot print the output of a currently executing program. Most programs, however, can "print" to a disk file that can be input to PRINT.

PRINT is a terminate-and-stay-resident (TSR) program. Once PRINT is loaded, you can load another program and execute it concurrently with PRINT. DOS executes both programs concurrently, allocating a defined buffer size and amount of time to the PRINT program. The syntax for three common uses of the PRINT command is given above.

The first form is used to initially load the PRINT program in RAM. This form lets you specify the device for printing, such as PRN or LPT1. If you do not specify a device name, DOS prompts you for one each time you execute the PRINT command. The first form also lets you define the buffer size (**/B**) and the amount of time (**/S**) allocated to printing. The maximum buffer size is 16,384 bytes (16KB) with a default of 512 bytes. Increasing the buffer size decreases the amount of RAM available for other programs, but may speed up printing. The maximum time slice is 255 slices per second, with a default of 2. Increasing the time slices can speed up printing but may slow the execution of other programs. If you want to use this form to change resource allocations, you must first restart DOS.

The second form of PRINT may be used as often as required to add or delete files to be printed from the print queue. Wildcard characters are allowed. The **/P** option adds the specified file(s) to the queue. The **/C** option removes (cancels) the specified file(s) from the queue. Files in the queue print on a first-in, first-out basis. You cannot change or remove a file while it is being printed with PRINT. In addition, you can't use the printer for another operation while PRINT is using it.

The last form of PRINT (**/T**) terminates all print jobs in the queue.

Examples of usage:

```
C:\DOS> PRINT /D:PRN /B:1024 /S:64
```
(installs PRINT with a buffer size of 1KB and 64 time slices)

```
C:\DOS> PRINT C:\SS\WORK1.PRN C:\ACCT\BUDGET.TXT /P
```
(adds two text files, WORK1.PRN and BUDGET.TXT, to the print queue)

```
C:\DOS> PRINT C:\SS\WORK2.PRN /P C:\ACCT\BUDGET.TXT /C
```
(adds WORK2.PRN to the print queue and removes BUDGET.TXT from the queue)

```
C:\DOS> print /t
```
(removes all files from the print queue)

SET Command (internal)

Syntax: `SET [variable=[string]]`

The **SET** command should be placed in the AUTOEXEC.BAT file to set any environment variables used by application programs each time you boot DOS. Many application programs use temporary work space on disk. Unless otherwise directed, these temporary files are stored in the current directory. When application programs experience problems during execution, the temporary work files may not get deleted. Disk management is easier when these work files are written to a specific directory, such as C:\TEMP.

To set an environment variable, use the SET command with an appropriate parameter, such as TEMP=C:\TEMP. To view the current environment, enter the SET command without any parameters. To clear a variable from the environment, enter the SET command with only the variable name and the equal sign.

Examples of usage:

```
C:\DOS> SET TEMP=C:\TEMP
```
(identifies the directory TEMP as the work space for any application program using TEMP as an environment variable)

C:\DOS> SET
(displays the current environment settings)

C:\DOS> SET TEMP=
(clears the TEMP variable from the environment)

SETVER (Set Version) Command (external)

Syntax: [d:][path]SETVER

or

[d:][path]SETVER filename n.nn

or

[d:][path]SETVER filename /D

The **SETVER** command allows you to add or remove program names from the DOS version table. This table identifies which version of DOS is reported for each program name in the table. Most programs run correctly with DOS 6, even if they were written to run with a previous version of DOS. Some programs execute only if DOS 6 makes them think that a certain version is running.

Before you can use this command to modify the DOS version table, the table must be loaded into RAM during the boot process. This is accomplished with the **DEVICE=SETVER.EXE** command in the CONFIG.SYS file. When you modify the table with SETVER, the changes are updated to a disk file, but the table in RAM is not changed. You must reboot after using SETVER to use the modified DOS version table.

The first form of SETVER (with no parameters) displays the DOS version table on the screen. You should pipe the output through the MORE filter (|MORE) to display one screen of output at a time.

The second form lets you add a filename with a desired version number to the DOS version table. Wildcard characters are not allowed. Suppose you want to execute a program (ACCT.EXE) that was designed to run with DOS 3.30 and does not run using DOS 6. To run ACCT.EXE with DOS 6, you must first modify the DOS version table by entering **SETVER ACCT.EXE 3.30.** Then, reboot to load the new DOS version table into RAM and run the program again. This technique will work for most older programs.

The last form of SETVER deletes a file from the DOS version table. In this form and the second form, only the filename is specified; a disk drive and path are not allowed. To remove ACCT.EXE from the table, enter **SETVER ACCT.EXE /D.**

Examples of usage:

`C:\DOS>` `SETVER | MORE`
(displays the contents of the current DOS version table on the screen, one screen at a time)

`C:\DOS>` `SETVER CALC4.EXE 3.01`
(adds CALC4.EXE to the table using DOS version 3.01)

`C:\DOS>` `setver calc4.exe /d`
(removes CALC4.EXE from the DOS version table on disk, but not in RAM)

SMARTDRV (Disk Caching) Command (external)

Syntax: `[d:][path]SMARTDRV [d:[+/-]] [/S]`

SMARTDRV is a disk caching program that decreases the time your computer spends reading data from your hard disk. No matter how fast today's disk drives are, they are slow when compared to RAM. With a disk caching program, reading and writing to disk goes through a RAM buffer area (cache) first. Every time your system requests information from the hard disk, the caching program intercepts this information and copies it to the cache. If the same information is needed again, it is taken from the cache instead of from the disk. Because accessing from RAM is much faster than accessing from disk, there is a substantial increase in performance. Thus, SMARTDRV should be in your AUTOEXEC.BAT file to run each time you boot.

The first megabyte (MB) of RAM is called conventional memory. Extended memory is that portion of RAM greater than 1MB. Memory is discussed in detail in Chapter 13. It is introduced here, because SMARTDRV uses extended memory for its disk cache. SMARTDRV cannot be run unless you have at least 1MB of RAM. By default, DOS sets the cache size based on the amount of extended memory available. For example, if you have 2–4MB of extended memory, SMARTDRV will set aside 1MB for the disk cache.

In addition to read-caching, SMARTDRV has write-caching. Write-caching captures the results of disk writes, and physically writes them to disk up to 5 seconds later. By delaying the write, multiple writes to the same area of the disk can often be executed as a single write, saving head movement time. However, write-caching can be potentially dangerous. Data stored in memory may never get written to disk if any of the following situations occur before the data is physically written to disk:

- The power goes off accidentally.

- Your application program hangs up.

- SMARTDRV encounters a fatal disk error.

Unless you have a significant need to improve the speed of writing data to disk, you should do read-caching, but not write-caching. DOS 6 has several options for specifying the drives to be cached and the type of caching.

The **[d:]** parameter specifies which drive you want to cache. If you don't specify any drives, DOS will default to the following:

- Your hard disk drives will be both read-cached and write-cached.

- Your floppy disks will be read-cached, but *not* write-cached.

You can specify multiple disk drives to be cached. For each drive you want cached, you may use the optional **[+/-]** parameter to tell SMARTDRV what type of caching you want:

- Use the plus (+) sign to enable both read-caching and write-caching for the specified drive.

- Use the minus (-) sign to disable all caching for the specified drive.

- Do not include either sign to enable read-caching and disable write-caching for the specified drive.

The **/S** option is used to view SMARTDRV statistics and see how effective it has been. Figure 12.3 shows you a sample statistics report.

Figure 12.3
Sample SMARTDRV
Statistics Report

```
Microsoft SMARTDrive Disk Cache version 5.0
Copyright 1991,1993 Microsoft Corp.


Room for  128 elements of  8,192 bytes each
There have been  303 cache hits
and  81 cache misses


Cache size: 1,048,576 bytes
Cache size while running Windows:  524,288 bytes


          Disk Caching Status
drive  read cache  write cache  buffering
-------------------------------------------
  A:       yes         no           no
  B:       yes         no           no
  C:       yes         yes          no


Write behind data will be committed before command prompt returns.
For help, type "Smartdrv /?".
```

This report was created using a system where SMARTDRV was run with no parameters or options. It shows the success rate of cache hits versus cache misses. A cache hit is where the system found what it was looking for in the cache, without having to access the disk. A cache miss is where it was forced to access the disk to complete the operation. Of course, the higher the hits, the more efficient the caching operation.

Figure 12.3 also shows the disk caching status of all disk drives. It shows that none of the disks used double buffering. Most hard disks do not need double buffering. To find out if your hard disk needs double buffering, you can add the /DOUBLE_BUFFER option (not shown above) to the end of the SMARTDRV command. Then, run MEMMAKER (covered in Chapter 13), followed by SMARTDRV /S. If every line in the "Buffering" column says "no," you do not need double buffering and the option can be removed. Use the **HELP SMARTDRV** command to find out more about disk caching.

Examples of usage:

C:\DOS> SMARTDRV
(a read/write disk cache is set up for all disks, using the disk caching settings shown in Figure 12.3)

C:\DOS> SMARTDRV C-
(a read-only disk cache is set up for Drive C only)

C:\DOS> smartdrv a- b- c+
(a read-only cache is created for the two floppy drives, and a read/write cache is created for the hard disk)

C:\DOS> SMARTDRV /S
(the SMARTDRV statistics report is displayed on the screen)

SYS (System) Command (external)

Syntax: [d:][path]SYS d:

SYS copies your DOS system files to another disk, such as a game disk. SYS transfers the hidden system files and COMMAND.COM to the drive designated, making the disk bootable. When you upgrade to DOS 6 from a previous version of DOS, the INSTALL command automatically transfers the DOS system files for you.

Examples of usage:

A:\> SYS B:
(transfers system files from Drive A to the disk in Drive B)

A:\> sys c:
(transfers system files from Drive A to the hard disk, Drive C)

Chapter 12

REVIEW
QUESTIONS

1. When should you execute the DBLSPACE command?

2. Why might you want more than one partition on your hard disk?

3. What is a TSR program?

4. How can you obtain a printed copy with detailed hardware information about your computer system?

5. How does a disk caching program work?

6. Why would it be a good idea to execute SMARTDRV in your AUTO-EXEC.BAT program if you have extended memory on your computer?

7. What is the purpose of the MODE command?

8. What does the command `MODE LPT1,8` do?

9. Specify the DOS command that increases the cursor speed to 50 percent faster than the default speed, keeping the delay for repeating characters unchanged.

10. What command changes a VGA screen to display 50 lines?

11. What must occur before MODE can be used to change the number of lines on the screen?

12. What is the purpose of the PRINT command?

13. What is the effect of varying PRINT buffer size and time slices?

14. What type of files can be printed using the PRINT command?

15. What DOS command lets you view the environment?

16. Why might you want to create a variable in the environment called TEMP?

17. What is the purpose of the SETVER command?

18. What steps in DOS 6 are required to make a program called WRITIT.EXE think it is being executed with DOS 3.20?

19. What is the purpose of the SYS command?

20. What files are transferred to the designated disk with the SYS command?

Chapter 12

FLOPPY DISK
LAB
EXERCISES

1. Create a batch file (**B:PRT132.BAT**) that lets you print any text on the printer with compressed print (132 characters per line). This would be useful for printing wide documents on 8 ½ × 11-inch paper. If your computer is attached to a printer, test the following batch file using a text file like AUTOEXEC.BAT as the replaceable parameter:

```
@ECHO OFF
REM PRT132.BAT TO PRINT COMPRESSED PRINT
REM PARAMETER USED IS THE TEXT FILE TO BE PRINTED
```

```
MODE LPT1 132
COPY %1 LPT1
MODE LPT1 80
```

2. Create a batch file (**B:KB.BAT**) that lets you experiment with the cursor speed and repeating key delay. Use EDIT to create the following batch file with two replaceable parameters:

```
@ECHO OFF
REM KB.BAT TO TEST KEYBOARD SPEEDS
MODE CON RATE=%1 DELAY=%2
```

When the batch file is correct, test it using different values for the replaceable parameters.

3. Execute the SET command without any parameters to view the environment. Then change the screen to display 40 characters per line and execute the SET command again to see the results. Now change the screen to display 80 characters per line and 43 lines per screen. Run the SET command with these changes. Return the screen back to 25 lines per screen when you are done.

4. Use the first form of SETVER to display the contents of your current DOS version table, pausing at the end of each screen. You can do this only if the table is loaded into RAM. If your instructor agrees, modify the table to include TEST.EXE with DOS 3.30. Reboot and display the modified contents of the table. When you are finished, use SETVER to remove TEST.EXE from the table.

5. Use the MSD command to create a report of hardware information about your computer. Write this report to a file on your data disk called HWINFO.TXT. Use EDIT to view the information in HWINFO.TXT.

6. Use the SMARTDRV/S command to view the existing status of disk caching.

This completes the Chapter 12 floppy disk lab exercises. Remove your disk(s) before you leave the computer.

Chapter 12

HARD DISK LAB EXERCISES

Follow the instructions for the floppy disk lab exercises 1–6 above with one exception: the files you create will be on Drive A, instead of Drive B.

This completes the Chapter 12 hard disk lab exercises. Remove your data disk before you leave the computer.

EXTENDED MEMORY MANAGEMENT

EXTENDED MEMORY MANAGEMENT

Windows applications and other "memory hungry" programs require more memory than was typically available in the past. This is why most computers purchased today have at least 4MB of RAM. However, no matter how much memory your computer has, DOS programs use only the first 640KB if not properly managed. Memory management programs are needed to effectively use memory past the first 640KB. DOS 6 includes these memory managers, plus commands that simplify the entire process of memory management.

The primary objectives of this chapter are to explain:

- The different types of RAM memory.

- How memory is managed to significantly improve the performance of any system with more than 1MB of RAM.

- Use of the MEM and MEMMAKER commands.

- Task swapping with extended memory.

TYPES OF RAM MEMORY

The subject of memory management becomes increasingly complex as the amount of available memory increases. Different types of RAM are used with today's more powerful PCs. The major memory types are called conventional, upper, and extended memory.

- The first 640KB of RAM is called **conventional memory**. This area is used for DOS commands and application programs. All versions of DOS use this area, and have since the 8088 microprocessor chip.

- Memory between 640KB and 1MB is called **upper memory**. Part of this area is used by system hardware, such as the display adapter. The rest of upper memory, referred to as upper memory blocks (UMBs), requires memory management commands to be used by DOS. **Note:** UMBs are available on 386 or 486 PCs, not 8088 or 286 PCs.

- The largest category of memory is called **extended memory**. When properly managed, it allows programs and data to be loaded above the DOS limit of 1MB. The first 64KB of extended memory is called high memory (HMA). It is used to load part of DOS, leaving more room in conventional memory for programs. The rest of extended memory, often called XMS memory, can be used for RAM disks, disk caching, and more.

The memory management programs discussed in this chapter allow all memory areas to be used more efficiently. Figure 13.1 identifies the memory areas available on a 386 or 486 PC.

Figure 13.1
Memory Allocation for 386 and 486 PCs

0		640KB		1MB		4096MB
Conventional Memory		Upper Memory		Extended Memory		
		Video		HMA	XMS Memory for:	
DOS 6	Application	Display	TSR	(64KB)		
System	Programs and	and	and	Rest of	• RAM disk	
Files	Working Data	ROM	Device	DOS and	• Disk caching	
		BIOS	Drivers	Buffers	• Print cache	

MEMORY MANAGEMENT FOR 286 PCS

If you have a 286 PC with extended memory, you can use memory management programs to free a significant amount of valuable space in conventional memory. Increasing the space for application programs has two benefits: you are able to run larger programs, and all programs execute faster.

If your PC has extended memory, part of DOS can be loaded in the high memory area. The following commands are required in your CONFIG.SYS file to load DOS in the high memory area:

```
DEVICE=C:\DOS\HIMEM.SYS
DOS=HIGH
BUFFERS=30
```

HIMEM.SYS is a system program that manages extended memory, including the high memory area. HIMEM.SYS lets application programs directly access memory above 1MB. It also configures the first 64KB of extended memory such that the HMA is addressable by DOS. The path (C:\DOS\) is typically included with the HIMEM.SYS command to load it from your hard disk.

DOS=HIGH allows a portion of DOS (including buffers) to be loaded in the HMA. DOS is an internal DOS command, so it does not require a path. HIMEM.SYS must be loaded with the CONFIG.SYS file to use the DOS=HIGH command. In addition, you must reboot DOS whenever you make changes to your CONFIG.SYS file.

BUFFERS is shown here because buffers can be assigned to the HMA, instead of conventional memory. With buffers and most of the command portion of DOS in the HMA, you can free about 60KB of conventional memory.

By default, DOS reserves the upper memory area for storing video driver programs and code from the ROM BIOS, which is the built-in part of DOS that controls basic input and output operations. However, with a 286 PC, Terminate-and-Stay-Resident (TSR) programs and device drivers must be loaded in conventional memory. They cannot be loaded in the upper memory area, as they can with 386 and 486 PCs (see Figure 13.1).

MEMORY MANAGEMENT FOR 386 AND 486 PCS

System performance can be increased significantly if you have a 386 or 486 PC with at least 2MB of RAM. In addition to loading DOS, you can load device drivers and TSR programs to the upper memory area. Further, you can create a RAM disk and a disk cache in extended memory, instead of in conventional memory. Commands for memory management are installed via entries in the CONFIG.SYS file, as shown in Figure 13.2.

Figure 13.2
Sample CONFIG.SYS File for Memory Management on a 386 or 486 PC

```
DEVICE=C:\DOS\HIMEM.SYS
DEVICE=C:\DOS\EMM386.EXE NOEMS HIGHSCAN
DOS=HIGH,UMB
DEVICEHIGH=C:\DOS\MOUSE.SYS
DEVICEHIGH=C:\DOS\RAMDRIVE.SYS 1024 /E
SHELL=C:\DOS\COMMAND.COM C:\DOS\ /E:2048 /P
BUFFERS=30
FILES=40
```

EMM386.EXE manages the upper memory area on 386 and 486 PCs. It makes sure that no two programs (or device drivers) use the same memory area at once. Like HIMEM.SYS, EMM386.EXE is loaded with the DEVICE command. A new **HIGHSCAN** option directs DOS to aggressively search the upper memory area for available space. This option can yield up to 64KB of additional memory. HIGHSCAN finds and uses the small upper memory blocks that remained unused in the past.

Expanded memory is additional memory installed on an expanded memory board. Because programs can only use expanded memory 64KB at a time, it is slower than extended memory. EMM386 can simulate expanded memory for programs that require it. If any application programs are designed to use expanded memory (EMS), change the **NOEMS** parameter of EMM386.EXE to **RAM**.

The **DOS=HIGH** command is modified slightly for a 386 or 486 PC. By adding the parameter **UMB** to the DOS command, you can load programs and device drivers into the upper memory blocks. Before you can use the UMB parameter, however, EMM386.EXE must be installed as shown above.

The **DEVICEHIGH** command loads device drivers in the upper memory area. In Figure 13.2, it installs a RAM disk (**RAMDRIVE.SYS**) in extended memory, using the **/E** option. Here, 1MB is allocated for the RAM disk. **Note:** If you have PC-DOS, use VDISK.SYS for the RAM disk.

In Figure 13.2, the SHELL, BUFFERS, and FILES commands are shown with recommended settings. The **SHELL** command tells DOS that the COMMAND.COM file is located on the DOS directory, not the root. Using the /E option, it increases the size of the environment from 64 bytes to a recommended size of 2048 bytes.

Getting the most out of your system with memory management is not always easy. Here are two potential problem areas to keep in mind:

- If any command or option locks up your system (e.g., HIGHSCAN), use the F8 key to do a selective boot and bypass the problem command. Then, use EDIT to fix the problem and reboot.

- Make sure your system always uses the latest versions of EMM386.EXE and HIMEM.SYS. Each time a new version of DOS or Windows is released, Microsoft updates EMM386.EXE and HIMEM.SYS.

  To locate the most recent version of EMM386.EXE on your hard disk: from the root directory, enter the command **DIR EMM386.EXE /S**. This command displays all occurrences of EMM386.EXE, including the date stamp. If multiple copies exist, make sure the path in the CONFIG.SYS file points to the directory with the most recent version.

In addition to using the CONFIG.SYS file to optimize memory, some changes may be required in your AUTOEXEC.BAT file. The sample AUTOEXEC.BAT file in Figure 13.3 shows these changes.

Figure 13.3

Sample AUTOEXEC.BAT File for Memory Management on 386 and 486 PCs

```
PROMPT $P$G
PATH D:\;C:\DOS;C:\WINDOWS;\C:\UTIL;\C:\MENU
LH C:\DOS\SMARTDRV.EXE
LH C:\DOS\GRAPHICS DESKJET C:\DOS\GRAPHICS.PRO
LH C:\DOS\PRINT
LH C:\DOS\DOSKEY
SET TEMP=D:\
MODE CON RATE=25 DELAY=1
REM LOAD WP AND 123 TO RAMDISK
COPY \WP51\WP.EXE D:
COPY \SS\123.* D:
REM EXECUTE MENU PROGRAM
CD\MENU
AUTO
```

LH (LOADHIGH) is an internal DOS command, which loads TSR programs in the upper memory area, rather than using conventional memory. Figure 13.3 shows four TSR programs loaded into upper memory with the LH command. **SMARTDRV.EXE** is the disk caching program DOS uses to improve disk processing. The **PRINT** command lets you execute other programs while printing disk files. **DOSKEY** retrieves previously entered commands from a buffer. These three TSR programs were covered in earlier chapters.

The **GRAPHICS** command improves the appearance of printed output when you use the PrtScr key to copy a screen display to the printer. Most printers print text characters correctly, but need help with graphics characters. DOS 6 provides the required translation tables (printer profiles) in a file named GRAPHICS.PRO. Use the **HELP GRAPHICS** command to find out what profiles are provided. The printer used in Figure 13.3 was an HP Deskjet.

With all the possibilities that exist for using conventional and upper memory areas, it is often necessary to see how efficiently memory is being used. This is where the MEM command comes in handy.

MEM Command

Syntax: `MEM [/C] [/P]`

The **MEM** command displays information about allocated memory areas, free memory areas, and programs currently loaded into memory. MEM can determine the effectiveness of your CONFIG.SYS and AUTOEXEC.BAT file entries. The **/C** option classifies how programs are loaded in memory, showing how much conventional and upper memory each program is using. The **/P** option pauses at the end of each screen, allowing time to view the information. Figure 13.4 shows a sample output of the MEM /C/P command after DOS was booted using entries similar to the previous CONFIG.SYS and AUTOEXEC.BAT files.

Refer to the section labeled "Modules using memory below 1MB:" in Figure 13.4. In this example, the total amount of conventional free memory is 618KB. This represents the largest application program you can run. The rest of conventional memory is required to store the RAM-resident portion of DOS 6. Figure 13.4 also shows that 135KB of upper memory is free. This is the amount of upper memory that could be used to load additional TSR programs and/or device drivers. More information on the MEM command is available with the **HELP MEM** command.

Figure 13.4
Screen Display of
MEM /C/P

```
Modules using memory below 1 MB:
  Name            Total      =  Conventional  + Upper Memory

  MSDOS         14,877   (15K)   14,877  (15K)        0   (0K)

  HIMEM          1,168    (1K)    1,168   (1K)        0   (0K)

  EMM386         3,120    (3K)    3,120   (3K)        0   (0K)

  COMMAND        2,992    (3K)    2,992   (3K)        0   (0K)

  MOUSE         14,016   (14K)        0   (0K)   14,016  (14K)

  RAMDRIVE       1,232    (1K)        0   (0K)    1,232   (1K)

  SMARTDRV      27,488   (27K)        0   (0K)   27,488  (27K)

  GRAPHICS       5,872    (6K)        0   (0K)    5,872   (6K)

  DOSKEY         4,144    (4K)        0   (0K)    4,144   (4K)

  Free         771,648  (754K)  633,040 (618K)  138,608 (135K)


Memory Summary:
  Type of Memory       Total      =      Used      +      Free

  Conventional        655,360           22,320           633,040

  Upper               191,360           52,752           138,608

  Reserved            393,216          393,216                 0

  Extended (XMS)    2,954,368        2,319,488           634,880


Press any key to continue . . .


  Total memory      4,194,304        2,787,776         1,406,528

  Total under 1 MB    846,720           75,072           771,648


  Largest executable program size           632,944    (618K)

  Largest free upper memory block           138,224    (135K)

  MS-DOS is resident in the high memory area.
```

The sample CONFIG.SYS and AUTOEXEC.BAT files presented in this chapter
are just the starting point for memory management. More complex entries are
available with DOS 6. MEMMAKER, covered next, is a wonderful command
that automatically fine-tunes existing memory management entries.

MEMMAKER
Command

Syntax: `MEMMAKER [/UNDO]`

The **MEMMAKER** command automatically reads most of the system information needed to modify your existing CONFIG.SYS and AUTOEXEC.BAT files so that device drivers and TSR programs load above the 640KB barrier. By varying the DEVICEHIGH and LH commands, MEMMAKER makes certain that all upper memory areas are used effectively. Do not delete, edit, or otherwise modify any changes MEMMAKER makes to your CONFIG.SYS and AUTOEXEC.BAT files. You must have at least a 386 PC to run MEMMAKER.

If you think MEMMAKER's memory configuration might be causing problems for your system, you can revert to your previous configuration. The **/UNDO** option will restore your CONFIG.SYS and AUTOEXEC.BAT files from backup files that MEMMAKER creates automatically.

When you run MEMMAKER, you will be prompted to run with either the *Express setup* or the *Custom setup*. When you specify Express Setup, MEMMAKER selects all the memory management options for you. We recommend you choose the Custom Setup so you can control some memory management options. Figure 13.5 lists the recommended responses to the Custom Setup if you plan on running DOS applications from Windows and have a color monitor. If you run only Windows applications (and no DOS applications), let DOS optimize upper memory for Windows by changing "No" to "Yes" in Figure 13.5.

Figure 13.5
Recommended Custom
Setup Options

```
                        Advanced Options
Specify which drivers and TSRs to include in optimization?  No
Scan the upper memory area aggressively?                    Yes
Optimize upper memory for use with Windows?                 No
Use monochrome region (B000-B7FF) for running programs?     Yes
Keep current EMM386 memory exclusions in inclusions?        Yes
Move Extended BIOS Data Area into upper memory?             Yes
```

To help MEMMAKER find the best configuration for optimizing memory, it creates a file called MEMMAKER.STS on your DOS directory. To view the statistics generated by MEMMAKER, use the **MORE<MEMMAKER.STS** command.

TASK SWAPPING WITH THE DOS SHELL

Another advantage of extended memory is being able to load multiple programs at once, and then switch between them without having to quit one program to load another. This process is called **task swapping**. For maximum efficiency, programs to be swapped should be loaded in extended memory.

Although task swapping is a feature of Windows, our discussion is confined to task swapping with DOS. It is available only through the DOSSHELL command. To enable task swapping with DOS, select the Options pull-down menu from the menu bar (Alt-O) and choose Enable Task Swapper (E). The Active Task List window appears in the lower right corner of the DOS shell screen, similar to Figure 13.6. This is where the names of active programs display. A RAM disk (Drive D) shows as a disk drive in the upper left corner of Figure 13.6.

Figure 13.6
DOS Shell Screen with
Active Task List

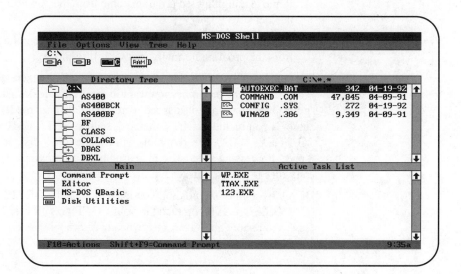

To add a program to the Active Task List:

1. Highlight a program file you wish to add.

2. Hold down the Shift key when you press the Enter key to select the program. This will add the program to the list, without actually starting it. The program will load when you switch to it.

3. Add as many programs to the Active Task List as you want.

To begin executing a program from the Active Task List:

1. Highlight the desired program name in the Active Task List.

2. Press the Enter key to execute the highlighted program.

3. If you have a mouse, you can double-click on a name in the Active Task List to execute that task.

To switch to a different program in the Active Task List:

1. Press Alt-Tab and continue to hold down the Alt key while you release the Tab key. You will temporarily exit the current program and the name of the next program appears at the top of the screen.

2. If this is the program you want to switch to, release the Alt key.

3. Otherwise, continue to hold the Alt key and press the Tab key to display the next program in the Active Task List.

4. When you switch back to a previous program, you will be put back into the program exactly where you left it.

To delete a program name from the Active Task List:

1. Remove a highlighted program name from the Active Task List by pressing the Del key.

2. A program name will be automatically deleted from the list when you exit from the program normally (not with swapping).

To make task swapping even faster and more efficient, create a RAM disk and copy to it all the programs you want in the Active Task List. Because many programs use temporary disk space, you should also use the RAM disk for this purpose. If you include a SET command, such as **SET TEMP=D:**, in your AUTOEXEC.BAT file, programs will use the RAM disk on Drive D for work space. Processing speeds are increased because programs keep track of temporary files in memory instead of on the hard disk.

If you have an EGA monitor, you must include the **DEVICEHIGH= C:\DOS\EGA.SYS** command in your CONFIG.SYS file. This enables DOS to save and restore an EGA screen when task swapping is used. It is not required for VGA monitors.

Chapter 13

REVIEW QUESTIONS

1. Explain the difference between conventional and extended memory.

2. What kinds of files are often placed in extended memory?

3. Why is it beneficial to load DOS to the high memory area?

4. What command loads DOS to the high memory area?

5. What three commands must precede the DEVICEHIGH command in a CONFIG.SYS file to provide access to the upper memory area?

6. What DOS command manages extended memory?

7. What DOS command loads device drivers in the upper memory area?

8. What is the benefit of using the HIGHSCAN option with HIMEM.SYS?

9. What DOS command can optimize your PC's memory?

10. What is the function of the MEMMAKER.STS file?

11. What is the purpose of the LH command?

12. Why should you use the LH command to install SMARTDRV.EXE?

13. What does the command **MEM/C/P** do?

14. Define the term *task swapping*.

15. What DOS command entered at the system prompt is required to enable task swapping?

16. How are programs added to the Active Task List?

17. How do you swap from the current program to another in the Active Task List?

18. What two ways can be used to remove programs from the Active Task List?

19. What purpose does the command **SET TEMP=D:** serve?

20. How are TSR programs loaded to the upper memory area?

Chapter 13

LAB EXERCISES

1. With DOS 6 you can view memory allocation a page at a time with the MEM/C/P command. However, the /P option was not available with DOS 5. Here is a way to simulate the /P option for the MEM command. This technique can be used with any DOS command in need of a pause option.

   Create a batch file on your data disk that redirects the output of the MEM/C command to a file viewed with the EDIT command. After creating **MEMORY.BAT** with the following commands, run it to see how it works:

   ```
   @ECHO OFF
   MEM/C > MEM.TMP
   EDIT MEM.TMP
   DEL MEM.TMP
   ```

2. Use EDIT to create a CONFIG.SYS file on Drive A that will install ANSI.SYS. Then, reboot DOS from Drive A. If you have a color monitor, change the screen to display red characters on a white background. If you have a VGA monitor, change the number of lines displayed to 43. Test these changes by displaying all the files on your DOS disk. Use MEMORY.BAT (from Exercise 1) to see where things are stored on your system.

3. Run the MEM /F command from the DOS shell.

This completes the Chapter 13 lab exercises. Remove your disk(s) before you leave the computer.

ADVANCED BATCH FILES

ADVANCED BATCH FILES

This chapter uses advanced batch file commands and techniques to create more powerful and useful batch files. The following commands are presented in this chapter:

IF   Allows for conditional branching within a batch file.

CHOICE Prompts users to make a choice within a batch file.

FOR   Repeats operations in a batch file.

CALL   Executes another batch file from within a batch file.

DEBUG Lets users view and/or create executable files.

BATCH FILE COMMANDS

IF Command

Syntax: `IF [NOT] condition GOTO location`

Suppose you have an accounting system that executes differently depending on the date (e.g., month-end or end of a quarter). **IF** instructs the batch file to execute differently, depending on specified conditions. When the condition specified is true, DOS branches to the specified GOTO location. Otherwise, the next command in the batch file is executed. The NOT condition is interpreted in reverse, branching only if the condition is false.

The IF command gives batch files the flexibility to branch depending on the various processing conditions that occur during execution. A GOTO command in the IF statement directs it to branch to another location in the batch file. Branch locations must include the colon as the first character of the name, such as :OK or :END. Branch locations are placed anywhere in the batch file. DOS uses the first eight characters to uniquely identify a branch location.

The most difficult part of using the IF statement is formulating the conditions that cause the desired branching. These conditions can be expressed in three different ways: **EXIST file**, **String1==String2**, and **ERRORLEVEL number**.

EXIST File Condition

If a data file required by a batch command does not exist, the **EXIST file** condition lets you modify the way the batch file executes. If the file exists (the EXIST file condition is true), the batch file can execute normally. Otherwise, appropriate measures may be taken to locate the correct file before proceeding. The following set of batch file commands verifies that a file exists before continuing:

```
:LOOP
IF EXIST A:FILEA.DOC GOTO OK
ECHO PUT CORRECT DISK IN DRIVE A
PAUSE
GOTO LOOP
:OK
```
(The remaining batch file commands would go here)

If A:FILEA.DOC is not found by DOS, the batch file pauses and directs the user to place the correct disk in Drive A. Then the GOTO command branches back to the location named LOOP to test for the existence of the file. If the file is found, the IF command executes the GOTO OK command, which branches around the error condition commands and begins executing the set of commands immediately following the location named :OK.

Using a replaceable parameter for the specified filename gives additional flexibility. For example, the IF statement in the previous example could have been: **IF EXIST A:%1 GOTO OK.**

You can also use the NOT EXIST condition with the IF command. Because all directories have a null file (by default), the following commands check for the existence of a given directory, represented here as a replaceable parameter:

```
IF NOT EXIST %1\NULL GOTO DOESNT
ECHO THE DIRECTORY %1 EXISTS
GOTO END
:DOESNT
ECHO THE DIRECTORY %1 DOES NOT EXIST
:END
```

Figure 14.1 shows a useful batch file that will execute a set of commands only if the date is a Friday. Here, the batch file only creates a work file (FRIDAY.TMP) on Fridays, based on the system date.

Figure 14.1
**Batch File to Execute
Commands Only on Friday**

```
@ECHO OFF
REM VER is piped to DATE so DATE executes without intervention.
VER | DATE | FIND "Fri" >DAY.TMP
REM DAY.TMP is created with no data filtered through FIND.
COPY DAY.TMP FRIDAY.TMP
REM The COPY command will not copy a file with zero bytes.
IF NOT EXIST FRIDAY.TMP GOTO END
DEL FRIDAY.TMP
ECHO IT IS FRIDAY!
(Place the Friday commands Here)
:END
DEL DAY.TMP
```

**String1 == String2
Condition**

When you execute a batch file with replaceable parameters, error checking is required to ensure the parameters are provided. DOS lets you check for missing parameters with the **String1==String2** condition. This condition evaluates as true when the two specified strings are identical. The double equal sign is required. Strings must be enclosed in quotation marks. The technique for using this condition is best explained with an example. If the second replaceable parameter is missing in a batch file, you can direct DOS to branch to another location with the following statement:

```
IF "%2"=="" GOTO ERR
```

In this example, String1 is the value of the replaceable parameter (%2). It is compared with String2, a null value (equal to nothing). When the batch file parameter is missing, the two strings are equal (nothing equals nothing), and the batch file branches to the location named ERR.

**ERRORLEVEL Number
Condition**

The **ERRORLEVEL number** condition evaluates as true when the previously executed batch file command has an error condition equal to or greater than the number specified. To see what errorlevel codes apply for a specific command, use on-line help (e.g., HELP FORMAT). Because errorlevel numbers vary by command, an ERRORLEVEL of 1 can signify an error. If an error has occurred, you can direct DOS to branch to the end of the batch file as follows:

```
IF ERRORLEVEL 1 GOTO END
```

This IF command directs DOS to branch GOTO to the :END location in the batch file whenever an error occurs. If ERRORLEVEL is zero (no errors), DOS executes the next batch file command in sequence.

CHOICE command

Syntax: CHOICE [/C:keystrokes] [/N] [text]

The **CHOICE** command prompts the user for a choice. After displaying the specified prompt, CHOICE pauses for the user to choose from a specified set of keystrokes. The **/C** option identifies the allowable keystrokes and displays them as part of the prompt. If the /C option is not used, CHOICE uses [Y/N] as the default. CHOICE supports only single-key input. The **/N** option directs CHOICE to *not* display the allowable choices.

When you want a brief explanation displayed with the allowable keystrokes, include it as optional text in the command. For example, the following command accepts only the numbers 1–4:

    CHOICE /C:1234 Enter the desired menu selection:

When executed, this CHOICE command displays on the screen as:

    Enter the desired menu selection:[1,2,3,4]?

To separate the acceptable choices [1,2,3,4] from the explanatory text, add a space after the text, at the end of the CHOICE command.

When executed, CHOICE sounds a warning beep if the user enters an invalid key. Errorlevel codes are set to indicate which key the user pressed. If the user pressed Ctrl-Break (or Ctrl-C), the errorlevel is 0. If the user entered the first allowable choice, the errorlevel is 1. If the user selected the second choice, the errorlevel is 2, and so on. When a fatal error occurs, the errorlevel is set to 255.

Because ERRORLEVEL is tested as being equal to or greater than a given value, the choices are often tested in decreasing order. For more information on CHOICE, use the **HELP CHOICE** command. Figure 14.2 shows how to use the CHOICE command with errorlevel codes to create your own menus.

Figure 14.2
Sample Batch File with
Choices

```
@ECHO OFF
:START
CLS
ECHO:
ECHO Main Menu Selections
ECHO:
ECHO 1. Word Processing
ECHO 2. Spreadsheets
ECHO 3. Database
ECHO:
ECHO E. Exit to system prompt
ECHO:
ECHO:
CHOICE /C:123E /N  Choose a menu option:
IF ERRORLEVEL 4 GOTO END
IF ERRORLEVEL 3 GOTO DB
IF ERRORLEVEL 2 GOTO SS
IF ERRORLEVEL 1 GOTO WP
GOTO END
:DB
CD\DBASE
DBASE
GOTO START
:SS
CD\LOTUS
123
GOTO START
:WP
CD\WP51
WP
GOTO START
:END
```

FOR Command

Syntax: `FOR %%v IN(set) DO command [command parameters]`

The FOR command runs a specified command for each file in a set of files. IN and DO are not parameters; they are required in the FOR command. The variable (*v*) is a one-letter name preceded by two percent signs (%%). The *set* specifies one or more files (or text strings) that you want to process with the specified command. Parentheses are required around the set, and values in the set must be separated by commas or spaces. The command executes with each successive value in the set by substituting the variable in the command with the set values. For example, the following batch file command deletes all BAK files in \WORD, \SS, and \HIST:

    FOR %%G IN(\WORD,\SS,\HIST) DO DEL %%G*.BAK

In this example, the three values in the set substitute for the variable "G" in the DEL command. It results in the following commands being executed:

    DEL \WORD*.BAK

    DEL \SS*.BAK

    DEL \HIST*.BAK

The **FOR** command adds significant capability to your batch files. It lets you perform a single DOS command on a group (or set) of filenames. This is very beneficial, because some DOS commands (like FIND and TYPE) do not accept wildcard characters. Wildcard characters can be used in the set. Without the capability of the FOR command, those DOS commands must be entered multiple times to be executed with multiple files.

Suppose you want to copy all of your files from one disk to another in sequence by filename extension. Specifically, you want to copy all COM files, then all EXE files, and finally, BAT files. You could create the following batch file called **KOPY.BAT:**

    @ECHO OFF

    FOR %%F IN (COM,EXE,BAT) DO COPY *.%%F B:

    ECHO COPY COMPLETE

You could have added flexibility by making the set of filename extensions replaceable parameters. In other words, you could substitute (%1,%2,%3) for (COM,EXE,BAT) in the FOR command. It is not mandatory that you use all of the replaceable parameters in a set. Using replaceable parameters, the command **KOPY DOC TXT** would copy all of the DOC files from the current directory to Drive B, followed by all TXT files. This would be identical to entering the following:

    COPY *.DOC B:

    COPY *.TXT B:

FOR also allows you to move down several levels of directories on your hard disk without having to find and enter the backslash key. Anyone who frequently uses different keyboards knows how frustrating it can be to locate the backslash key. To avoid this problem, enter the following command in a batch file called **TO.BAT**:

```
FOR %%X IN (\%1,%2,%3,%4) DO CD %%X
```

Be sure to place this batch file in a directory that is specified in your current search path, so DOS can find it from any directory. To change to \WORD\MEMOS\HIST from any subdirectory on the hard disk, enter **TO WORD MEMOS HIST**. In effect, this would execute the CD command three times as follows:

```
CD \WORD

CD MEMOS

CD HIST
```

The FOR command is also entered interactively at the DOS system prompt. When the FOR variable is entered from the system prompt, only one % is used to identify the variable name. For example, to print the contents of all batch files on Drive B, you could execute the following FOR command at the system prompt:

```
A:\> for %x in (b:*.bat) do type %x >prn
```

CALL Command

Syntax: `CALL [d:][path] filename [parameters]`

Batch files can be executed from within a batch file. However, when you include just the batch file name for execution, DOS transfers control to that batch file with no way to return to the original batch file. This is all right if the batch file to which you want to transfer is the last command in the original batch file. It becomes a problem if there are other commands to execute in the original batch file. The **CALL** command resolves this problem by returning to the next command in the first batch file after executing the second batch file.

Use CALL to execute another batch file from within the original batch file. You can also include any parameters required by that batch file. When the "called" batch file is finished, DOS continues processing the remaining commands in the original batch file. In the following example, when the batch file DOACCT.BAT is finished, the remaining commands in the original batch file are executed.

```
PAUSE PLACE ACCOUNTING DATA DISK IN DRIVE A

CALL DOACCT
```

(Commands to be executed after DOACCT.BAT)

CREATING EFFECTIVE BATCH FILES

What is an effective batch file? Any batch file that improves your ability to be productive and minimizes errors is a likely candidate. Here we cover several ways to create effective batch files.

One technique is to create batch files that give you added protection from making a mistake. For example, when you want to delete a group of files using wildcard characters, you should always display a list of the files you want to delete before you delete them. The batch file (PURGE.BAT) in Figure 14.3 demonstrates this technique. It is an effective substitute for the DEL command.

Figure 14.3
Batch File to Display
Files Being Deleted

```
@ECHO OFF
REM IMPROVED DEL COMMAND (PURGE.BAT)
DIR %1/W
ECHO THESE FILES WILL BE DELETED (PRESS CTRL-BREAK TO ABORT)
PAUSE
DEL %1
```

Another technique is to create a batch file that will automatically respond to DOS prompts. For example, when you format a disk, change the volume label, or delete all files on a directory, DOS requests information to continue. If you want to automatically enter a single response, you can use ECHO to pipe a response to a DOS command. The following command automatically deletes all files on the default directory without waiting for a response to the "Are you sure?" message:

```
ECHO Y | DEL *.* >NUL
```

The screen output "Are you sure (Y/N)?" is redirected to NUL so it is not displayed on the screen during the delete operation. If you have multiple responses to a DOS command in a batch file, you must use a different technique.

To automatically enter multiple responses in a batch file, you can create a text file containing the responses and redirect it to a DOS command. Suppose you wanted to FORMAT a single data disk with the volume label DATADISK. Using EDIT, you can create a file called RESP.DAT as follows:

```
<Enter>
DATADISK<Enter>
N<Enter>
```

This text file contains the responses necessary to automatically execute the FOR-MAT command. The first response (just an Enter key) tells DOS that the disk is in the drive and ready to be formatted. The next response supplies the volume label. The last response tells DOS that there are no more disks to be formatted. Redirection is used to input responses to the FORMAT command when needed. The following batch file commands can then be used to format a data disk automatically:

```
ECHO PLACE DISK TO BE FORMATTED IN DRIVE %1
PAUSE
FORMAT %1 <RESP.DAT
```

It is also very important that batch files detect errors, especially when replacement parameters are used. Suppose you want a batch file that restricts the user to formatting only Drive A. In other words, you want to control the way FORMAT executes. First, you must rename FORMAT.COM to something else, like FORM.COM. Then you can create a batch file (**FORMAT.BAT**) that executes whenever FORMAT is entered as a command. Figure 14.4 shows the commands in FORMAT.BAT. Whenever you enter FORMAT and the first parameter is missing, or is other than A: or a:, it is rejected by this batch file.

Figure 14.4
Batch File to Format Drive A Only

```
@ECHO OFF
REM FORMAT.BAT TO FORMAT ONLY DRIVE A
IF "%1"=="" GOTO ERROR
IF %1==A: GOTO OK
IF %1==a: GOTO OK
ECHO YOU ARE NOT ALLOWED TO FORMAT DRIVE %1
GOTO END
:OK
REM A SECOND REPLACEABLE PARAMETER LETS
REM YOU INCLUDE OPTIONS LIKE /F:720
FORM %1 %2
GOTO END
:ERROR
ECHO YOU MUST ENTER THE DRIVE TO FORMAT
:END
```

To prevent newly installed programs from changing your AUTOEXEC.BAT file without your knowledge, place your automatic execution commands in another batch file, such as ALIAS.BAT. Then include only two lines in your AUTOEXEC.BAT file as follows:

```
@ECHO OFF
ALIAS.BAT
```

DEBUG COMMAND

DEBUG is a machine-level utility program for snooping around in DOS and making all sorts of subtle modifications. In addition to creating executable programs, it can display memory values, modify them, and view executable files like those with EXE or COM extensions. If you know what you are doing, you can use DEBUG to recover lost disk files and edit the COMMAND.COM file. In fact, a whole chapter could be devoted to this extraordinary command. Our intent, however, is to introduce you to DEBUG, not to make you a DEBUG expert!

You can use DEBUG to view the contents of an executable file. To view the contents of the FORMAT command, enter **DEBUG FORMAT.COM**. The first thing you would see displayed on the screen is the hyphen (-), which is the DEBUG command prompt. Enter the DEBUG command **D** to display 128 bytes of the file. Figure 14.5 shows you what the screen might look like after you pressed the D key twice.

Figure 14.5
Screen Display of DEBUG

```
C:\DOS>debug format.com
-d
2043:0100  B8 23 AA BA C2 57 3B C4-73 69 8B C4 2D 44 03 90   .#...W:.si..-D..
2043:0110  25 F0 FF 8B F8 B9 A2 00-90 BE 7E 01 FC F3 A5 8B   %.........~....
2043:0120  D8 B1 04 D3 EB 8C D9 03-D9 53 33 DB 53 CB 0E 01   .........S3.S...
2043:0130  50 4B 4C 49 54 45 20 43-6F 70 72 2E 20 31 39 39   PKLITE Copr. 199
2043:0140  32 20 50 4B 57 41 52 45-20 49 6E 63 2E 20 41 6C   2 PKWARE Inc. Al
2043:0150  6C 20 52 69 67 68 74 73-20 52 65 73 65 72 76 65   l Rights Reserve
2043:0160  64 4E 6F 74 20 65 6E 6F-75 67 68 20 6D 65 6D 6F   dNot enough memo
2043:0170  72 79 24 B8 00 09 BA 61-01 CD 21 CD 20 90 FD 8B   ry$....a..!. ...
-d
2043:0180  F8 4F 4F BE C0 02 03 F2-8B CA D1 E9 F3 A5 FC 87   .OO.............
2043:0190  F7 46 46 BF 00 01 AD 95-BA 10 00 EB 32 90 AD 95   .FF.........2...
2043:01A0  B2 10 EB 3B AD 95 B2 10-EB 3C AD 95 B2 10 EB 41   ...;.....<.....A
2043:01B0  AD 95 B2 10 EB 63 AD 95-B2 10 EB 64 AD 95 B2 10   .....c.....d....
2043:01C0  EB 65 AD 95 B2 10 EB 66-AD 95 B2 10 72 08 A4 D1   .e.....f....r...
2043:01D0  ED 4A 74 F4 73 FB 33 C9-33 DB D1 ED 4A 74 BF D1   .Jt.s.3.3...Jt..
2043:01E0  D3 D1 ED 4A 74 BE D1 D3-85 DB 74 17 D1 ED 4A 74   ...Jt.....t...Jt
2043:01F0  B9 D1 D3 80 FB 06 72 0B-D1 ED 4A 75 04 AD 95 B2   ......r...Ju....
-
```

The DEBUG display is in two parts. The left side displays the data in hexadecimal (base 16) form and the right side shows the character translations in ASCII. Continue to press D to display more of the file. Use the DEBUG command **Q** (Quit) to exit DEBUG.

Because DEBUG is provided for advanced DOS users, novice users typically find it too technical and complicated. But don't get discouraged. You can find detailed instructions on how to use DEBUG in the DOS technical manual and other reference works. Figure 14.6 contains the DEBUG instructions for creating an executable program to capture a keystroke, such as a one-character password. The explanatory text, enclosed in parentheses, is not keyed.

Figure 14.6
DEBUG Commands to Create GETKEY.COM

```
DEBUG                          (Execute the DEBUG command)
-E 100 B4 00 CD 16 B4 4C CD 21 (Enter instructions)
-N GETKEY.COM                  (Name the executable program GETKEY.COM)
-RCX                           (Change the size Register, CX)
:8                             (Set the size to 8 bytes)
-W                             (Write the new file to disk)
-Q                             (Quit DEBUG)
```

After GETKEY.COM is created, you can use it in a batch file to identify a keystroke from a user. Strange as it may seem, errorlevel codes are used to identify a keystroke entered with the GETKEY program. Most errorlevel codes are shown in Figure 14.7.

Figure 14.7
Sample Errorlevel Codes

```
    0 = NUL
    7 = Bell (Ctrl-G)
   13 = Enter key
   27 = Esc key
   32 = Space bar
48-57 = Digits (0-9)
   63 = Question mark (?)
65-90 = Uppercase alphabet (A-Z)
97-122 = Lowercase alphabet (a-z)
```

When testing for a specific errorlevel code with the IF command, DOS looks for a code equal to or greater than the code specified to evaluate the condition as true. For example, to identify the ? key (ERRORLEVEL 63), you must test for a code that is 63 or more, but not 64 or more. Figure 14.8 shows a batch file you can create and test to see how errorlevel testing works.

Figure 14.8
Example of Errorlevel Testing

```
@ECHO OFF
:TOP
ECHO BREAK OUT OF THIS LOOP BY PRESSING THE ? KEY ONLY
GETKEY
IF ERRORLEVEL 63 IF NOT ERRORLEVEL 64 GOTO CONT
GOTO TOP
:CONT
```

Although batch file processing adds power and convenience to the operation of a computer, it is not a replacement for a programming language, such as C or BASIC. DOS batch files execute rather slowly, because each command is interpreted by DOS during execution. However, for the user who doesn't want to spend the time to learn a programming language, batch files offer a useful alternative.

Chapter 14

REVIEW QUESTIONS

1. What is the main purpose of the IF statement in a batch file?
2. What does a GOTO statement do in a batch file?
3. How do you identify a location to branch to in a batch file?
4. What does the EXIST file condition let you do in a batch file?
5. What does an ERRORLEVEL code of zero mean?
6. How can a batch file detect a missing replaceable parameter?
7. Explain how the FOR command works.
8. What FOR command deletes all BAK and TMP files in the current directory?
9. When can wildcard characters be used in the FOR command?
10. What does the command **FOR %x IN (*.BAT) DO FIND "PATH" %x** do?
11. What is the purpose of the CALL command?
12. How can you automatically enter a single predefined response to a DOS command in a batch file?

13. How can you automatically enter multiple predefined responses to a DOS command in a batch file?

14. Under what specific conditions would DOS be able to execute a batch file named CHKDSK.BAT?

15. What happens when you redirect screen output to NUL?

16. Specify the IF command used after GETKEY.COM to branch to a location named END when the number 1 is entered from the keyboard.

17. What are three things you can do with the DEBUG command?

18. What happens when the following commands are executed in a batch file?

```
CHOICE Defrag Drive C

IF ERRORLEVEL 2 GOTO SKIP

DEFRAG C:

:SKIP
```

19. How is the FOR command executed in a batch file differently than from the system prompt?

20. List the batch file command(s) that will delete all the BAK files from up to five given directories on Drive C.

Chapter 14

FLOPPY DISK LAB EXERCISES

1. Instead of purchasing a utility program to search your hard disk for a particular filename, you can create your own customized batch file named PHIND.BAT. You cannot call this file FIND.BAT because entering the batch file name of FIND would cause DOS to execute FIND.COM. Create the following batch file (without the explanatory comments):

`@ECHO OFF`	(Turn echo off)
`IF "%1"=="" GOTO ERROR`	(If no parameter, branch to ERROR)
`CHKDSK B:/V ¦ FIND "%1"`	(Send all filenames on Drive B to filter)
`GOTO END`	(Branch around the error message to END)
`:ERROR`	(Branch location labeled ERROR)
`ECHO PARAMETER REQUIRED`	(Display error message)
`:END`	(Branch location labeled END)

This useful batch file directs CHKDSK to locate every filename on Drive B and pipe the names to FIND. FIND filters out all filenames not containing the characters specified by the variable parameter (%1). The IF test lets the batch file skip over the CHKDSK and FIND operations if no parameter is included with PHIND. Figure 14.9 shows what the screen might look like if you executed PHIND.BAT, first with no parameter, and then with TEST as a parameter.

Figure 14.9

Screen Display After Executing PHIND.BAT

```
C:\DOS>phind TEST
B:\TEST.1
B:\TEST.3
B:\TEST.4
B:\TEST.ROF
B:\TEST1.DIR
B:\TESTZ.DIR
B:\TESTS.DIR
C:\DOS>
```

2. Create the following batch file called SUPERMAT.BAT that will format a disk with the /S option and automatically copy FORMAT.COM and CHK-DSK.COM to the newly formatted disk. This would be a useful program for formatting floppy disks that are bootable and contain the FORMAT and CHKDSK commands. Specific application programs could also be copied to these bootable disks. If you have a blank disk, execute this program to see how it works.

```
@ECHO OFF
REM SUPERMAT.BAT USED TO CREATE BOOTABLE DISKS
CLS
FORMAT B:/S
COPY FORMAT.COM B: >NUL
COPY CHKDSK.COM B: >NUL
DIR B:
ECHO END OF SUPERMAT
```

3. The EDIT command in DOS does not automatically create a backup copy of the original file before it is modified. To overcome this limitation, create a simple batch file as follows:

- First, rename EDIT.COM to EDYT.COM.

- Create a batch file named EDIT.BAT with these two lines:

```
COPY %1.%2 %1.BAK
EDYT %1.%2
```

- To edit a file, enter the command EDIT with two replaceable parameters. The first parameter must be the filename, and the second parameter must be the filename extension. Thus, to edit SUPERMAT.BAT and have the original file saved as SUPERMAT.BAK, enter:

```
EDIT SUPERMAT BAT
```

When you are finished testing EDIT.BAT, rename EDYT.COM back to EDIT.COM and delete EDIT.BAT.

4. Use the following DEBUG commands to create an executable program that sends a form feed (FF) control character to an IBM- or Epson-compatible printer:

```
-N FF.COM
-E 0100 B4 05 B2 0C CD 21 CD 20
-RCX
:8
-W
-Q
```

If you are connected on-line to an IBM- or Epson-compatible printer, test your new command by entering **FF** at the system prompt. Your printer should advance to the top of the next page.

5. Sometimes users want protection against other users, particularly from novice users, accessing their system without permission. Although few protection systems can deter an experienced user, the batch file in Figure 14.10 will help. When these commands are placed in the beginning of your AUTOEXEC.BAT file, novice users will be unlikely to get through the boot process without entering the correct password.

Figure 14.10
Password Protection
Batch File

```
@ECHO OFF
REM PASSWORD PROTECTION
PROMPT Fatal Disk Error #23 — Reboot
:TOP
CLS
ECHO Unrecoverable read error on Drive A:
ECHO Abort, Retry, or Fail?
GETKEY
IF ERRORLEVEL 63 IF NOT ERRORLEVEL 64 GOTO END
:CAUSE THE DISK TO SPIN FOR A WHILE
COPY COMMAND.COM COMMAND.BAK >NUL
DEL COMMAND.BAK
GOTO TOP
:END
(Place rest of AUTOEXEC.BAT commands here)
```

Have you figured out the purpose of the PROMPT command in this batch file yet? If you halt execution of the batch file with Ctrl-Break, the reason may become evident to you.

This concludes the Chapter 14 floppy disk lab exercises. Remove your disk(s) before you leave the computer. We hope you enjoyed learning DOS and doing the exercises in this text. Best wishes for better computing!

Chapter 14

HARD DISK LAB EXERCISES

Follow the instructions for the floppy disk lab exercises above, making the following changes where applicable:

- Change Drive B (data disk) to Drive A in the first two batch files (PHIND.BAT and SUPERMAT.BAT).
- Change Drive A (DOS disk) to Drive C in the last exercise.

This concludes the Chapter 14 hard disk lab exercises. Remove your data disk before leaving the computer. We hope you enjoyed learning DOS and doing the exercises in this text. Best wishes for better computing!

SUMMARY OF DOS COMMANDS

This list includes commands covered in the text and others that you might need to use.

Command	Ver.	Chapter	Brief Description of Command
APPEND	3.2	—	Sets a search path for data files.
ATTRIB	3.0	6	Sets/displays file attributes.
CD	2.0	7	Changes directories (CHDIR).
CHKDSK	1.0	6	Checks for file fragmentation on a disk.
CLS	2.0	5	Clears the screen.
COMMAND	1.0	—	Supplies internal DOS commands.
COPY	1.0	5	Copies specified files.
DATE	1.1	5	Displays and sets the system date.
DBLSPACE	6.0	12	Data compression program.
DEBUG	2.0	14	Machine-level utility program.
DEFRAG	6.0	8	Defragments a disk.
DEL	1.0	5	Deletes (erases) specified files.
DELTREE	6.0	7	Deletes both files and directories.
DIR	1.0	5	Displays directory entries.
DISKCOMP	1.0	—	Compares two floppy disks.
DISKCOPY	1.0	6	Makes an exact copy of a disk.
DOSKEY	5.0	9	Recalls and edits previous commands.
DOSSHELL	4.0	4	Starts the graphical interface to DOS.
EDIT	5.0	10	Executes the DOS full-screen editor.
EMM386	5.0	13	Extended memory manager.
ERASE	1.0	5	Identical to DELETE command.

EXIT	2.0	4	Exits DOS and returns to an application program.
EXPAND	6.0	—	Expands DOS files during installation.
FASTOPEN	3.3	—	Improves hard disk performance.
FDISK	2.0	12	Partitions a hard disk for DOS.
FIND	2.0	9	Searches for a given string of text.
FORMAT	1.0	3	Formats a disk to receive DOS files.
GRAPHICS	2.0	13	Prepares DOS for printing graphics.
HELP	5.0	3	Provides on-line help for DOS.
INTERLNK	6.0	—	Links computers to share resources.
LABEL	3.0	6	Labels a disk.
LH	5.0	13	Loads TSR programs into high memory.
MD	2.0	7	Makes a directory (MKDIR).
MEM	4.0	13	Displays amount of used and free memory.
MEMMAKER	6.0	13	Optimizes memory management.
MODE	1.0	12	Modifies system device parameters.
MORE	2.0	9	Displays output one screen at a time.
MOVE	6.0	7	Moves files and/or directories.
MSAV	6.0	8	Microsoft anti-virus program.
MSBACKUP	6.0	8	Microsoft backup and restore program.
MSD	6.0	12	Microsoft system diagnostic program.
MWAV	6.0	8	Windows version of MSAV.
MWBACKUP	6.0	8	Windows version of MSBACKUP.
MWUNDEL	6.0	8	Windows version of UNDELETE.
PATH	2.0	7	Sets a command search path.
PRINT	2.0	12	Prints a file concurrently.

PROMPT	2.0	7	Assigns the system prompt.
RD	2.0	7	Removes a directory (RMDIR).
REN	1.0	5	Renames files (RENAME).
REPLACE	3.2	—	Facilitates updating of files.
SET	2.0	12	Sets DOS environment variables.
SETVER	5.0	12	Controls what version number is reported.
SCANDISK	6.2	8	Detects and repairs disk errors.
SMARTDRV	6.0	12	Creates a disk cache.
SORT	2.0	9	Sorts data forward or backward.
SUBST	3.1	—	Substitutes a string for a pathname.
SYS	1.0	12	Transfers DOS system files to a disk.
TIME	1.0	5	Displays and sets the system time.
TREE	2.0	7	Displays directories and filenames.
TYPE	1.0	5	Displays contents of a file.
UNDELETE	5.0	6	Recovers accidentally deleted files.
UNFORMAT	5.0	—	Restores a disk erased by FORMAT.
VER	2.0	5	Displays the DOS version number.
VERIFY	2.0	—	Verifies all writes to a disk.
VOL	2.0	5	Displays the disk volume label.
VSAFE	6.0	—	RAM-resident virus safety utility.
XCOPY	3.2	6	Expanded version of the COPY command.

DOS Configuration File Commands	Command	Chapter	Brief Description of Command
	BREAK	11	Sets or clears extended Ctrl-Break checking.
	BUFFERS	11	Allocates memory for disk buffers.
	DEVICE	11	Loads a device driver in conventional memory.
	DEVICEHIGH	13	Loads a device driver in the high memory area.
	DOS	13	Loads part of DOS in the high memory area.
	DRIVPARM	—	Modifies the parameters of an existing drive.
	FILES	11	Sets the number of files DOS can access at a time.
	LASTDRIVE	—	Specifies the maximum number of disk drives.
	SHELL	11	Increases the size of the DOS environment.
	STACKS	—	Increases the size of the stack areas.

DOS Device Driver Commands	Command	Chapter	Brief Description of Command
	ANSI.SYS	11	Used to change screens and keyboards.
	DISPLAY.SYS	—	Supports code-page switching for the console.
	DRIVER.SYS	—	Specifies parameters for a nonsupported drive.
	EGA.SYS	13	Restores display when task swapper is used.
	HIMEM.SYS	13	Manages the use of extended memory.
	PRINTER.SYS	—	Supports code-page switching for printers.
	RAMDRIVE.SYS	11	Creates a RAM disk in memory.

DOS Batch File Commands

Command	Chapter	Brief Description of Command
CALL	14	Executes another batch file.
CHOICE	14	Waits for a certain key to be pressed.
ECHO	10	Sets the batch file echo feature on/off.
FOR	14	Command for repetitive looping.
GOTO	14	Command for branching.
IF	14	Command for conditional branching.
PAUSE	10	Pauses for operator action.
REM	10	Provides for remarks or comments.

COMMON DOS ERROR MESSAGES

Abort, Retry, Fail?
A disk error has occurred. Enter A to end (abort) the task that requested the disk operation. Enter R to retry the operation if you think that the error might not happen again, or you have corrected the problem (for example, closing the drive latch or reinserting the disk). Press F to end the operation, but continue the task that requested the disk operation.

Access denied
You tried to modify a write-protected or read-only file. Modify the file attributes to gain access.

ANSI.SYS must be installed
You tried to execute a command (like MODE) that uses the ANSI.SYS device driver. Install ANSI.SYS in the CONFIG.SYS file and reboot.

Bad command or filename
The command entered is not a valid DOS command, or DOS cannot find the command. Check for correct path.

Bad or missing Command Interpreter
COMMAND.COM is not on the root directory of the boot disk. Enter the correct path and name for command interpreter (e.g., C:\DOS\COMMAND.COM).

Data error reading (or writing) disk
The disk in the specified drive has a bad sector. If entering R (retry) does not resolve the problem, enter A to abort the process.

Directory already exists
You attempted to create a directory using an existing directory name. Use a different name or a different path for the new directory.

Disk unsuitable for system disk
FORMAT detected a bad track on the disk where the system resides. The disk can possibly be formatted as a nonsystem disk.

Duplicate filename or file not found
You used the REN command to rename a file and either you specified a new name that already exists, or DOS cannot find the file you wish to rename.

File allocation table bad

The disk may be defective. Run CHKDSK /F to fix the problem. If the fix is unsuccessful, you must reformat the disk.

File cannot be copied onto itself

The source filename is the same as the target filename. Make sure the filenames, including the disk drive and path, are different.

File creation error

You tried to add a filename that already exists in the directory, or there was not enough space for the file.

File not found

DOS could not find any file(s) that match the name(s) you provided.

Format failure

A fatal disk error prevented DOS from formatting the disk. Try another disk.

Incorrect DOS version

You attempted to run a DOS command from a DOS version different from that used to boot the system. Re-enter the DOS command for the version of DOS used to boot the system. Also, see SETVER command.

Insufficient disk space

The disk does not have enough space available to perform the specified operation.

Internal stack overflow

You need to increase the size and/or number of stacks using the STACKS command in the CONFIG.SYS file.

Invalid drive specification

You specified a nonexistent disk drive in a command. Correct the drive identification and re-enter the command.

Invalid media, track 0 bad or unusable

Track zero on the disk to be formatted is unusable. Either it is corrupted or the density type is not correct.

Invalid number of parameters

The command line entered did not contain the correct number of parameters for the command invoked. For example, it might have had an extra delimiter.

Invalid parameter(s)	One of the specified command options is wrong or does not exist.
Invalid path, not directory, or directory not empty	You could not remove a directory for one of the specified reasons. Correct the problem and re-enter the command.
Lost allocation units found in chains	The FAT has allocation units marked as used by a file, but there are no directory entries that use those allocation units (see CHKDSK).
Non-system disk or disk error	The default disk is not a bootable DOS disk. If you have a floppy disk in Drive A on a hard disk system, most PCs will boot from the floppy disk.
Not ready error reading drive X	DOS cannot read or write to the specified drive. Correct the problem and enter R to retry. If the problem cannot be fixed, enter A to abort the operation.
Out of environment space	The total space required for all SET commands exceeds the size of the environment. Increase the space with the SHELL command in the CONFIG.SYS file.
Path not found	One of the directory names in the path you provided does not exist.
Program too big to fit in memory	DOS cannot load an executable program because of insufficient free space. Remove any unnecessary buffers and TSR programs and try again.
Required parameter missing	You failed to supply a parameter required to execute the command.
Sector not found	DOS was unable to locate all of the sectors for a disk file due to a corrupted File Allocation Table or bad disk (see CHKDSK).

Target diskette may be unusable

The target disk in a DISKCOPY operation has an unrecognizable format or it is defective.

This disk cannot be unformatted Proceed with Format (Y/N)?

The diskette you are trying to format is too full for FORMAT to add its MIRROR file. If you respond "Y", the disk will format correctly, but you won't be able to unformat the disk later.

Too many parameters

You supplied too many parameters for a command. Often this is due to extra spaces in a filename.

Write fault error writing device prn

The printer cannot receive data. Make sure the printer is connected (on-line) and in a "ready" status, then press R to retry the operation.

Write protect error

You tried to write data to a disk with a tab covering the write-protect notch, or the disk does not have a notch, which also protects the data it contains.